# ATTILA CONQUERS

# AMERICA, INC.

"Fantastic!"
—**Tom Peters, coauthor of** *In Search of Excellence*

➤

"Powerful and inspiring! Will help you make the most of your leadership potential."
—**Wayne W. Dyer, Ph.D.,**
  **author of** *Your Erroneous Zones*

➤

"Delightful!"
—**William K. Coors, chairman,**
  **Adolph Coors Company**

➤

"Superb, thought-provoking! Entertaining and easy to read, yet acutely relevant to anyone in a leadership position... packed with many layers of wisdom."
—**Scott DeGarmo, editor in chief,** *Success*

➤

"One of the most original and inspiring books on leadership I've encountered."
—**Robert Schuller, author of**
  ***Tough Times Don't Last but Tough People Do!***
  **and** *The Be-Happy Attitudes*

➤

"Don't let the title mislead you! This brilliant leadership masterpiece is relevant, inspirational, laser-accurate and full of win-win wisdom atypical of Attila's image. Easy to read... impossible to forget!"
—**Denis Waitley, Ph.D., author of**
  *The Psychology of Winning*
  **and** *Seeds of Greatness*

➤

"It's a great point of view about another way to show leadership...very, very impressive. I will be using many of the author's ideas in my own work."
—**Pat Riley, coach, Los Angeles Lakers**

"*Leadership Secrets of Attila the Hun* captures elegantly the time-tested principles of leadership. A must reading for today's managers, this book energizes individuals to realize their leadership potential."
—**Dr. Ram Charan, coauthor of *Strategic Management* and contributor to the *Harvard Business Review***

"Having had the good fortune to associate my own book on management with the name of a saint, never would I have imagined Attila could offer such sage and readable advice.... This is recommended reading."
—**Norman R. Augustine, chairman and CEO, Martin Marietta Corporation, and author of *Augustine's Laws***

"An unusual approach to presenting solid content...most helpful to anyone who wants to grow and develop effective leadership skills."
—**Nido R. Qubein, chairman, Creative Services, Inc.**

"Attila could well lead any corporation today."
—**Andrew P. Calhoun, Jr., chairman, The Resource Group**

"Worth reading...could be the most popular management book since *The One-Minute Manager*."
—*Memphis Business Journal*

# LEADERSHIP SECRETS OF ATTILA THE HUN

## WESS ROBERTS, Ph.D.

WARNER BOOKS

A Warner Communications Company

Copyright © 1985, 1987 by Wess Roberts
All rights reserved

Warner Books, Inc., 666 Fifth Avenue, New York, NY 10103

Printed in the United States Of America
First trade printing February 1990
10 9 8 7 6 5 4 3

**W** A Warner Communications Company

**Library of Congress Cataloging in Publication Data**

Roberts, Wess.
  Leadership secrets of Attila the Hun / by Wess Roberts.
     p.  cm.
  ISBN 0-446-39106-9 (pbk.) (U.S. and Canada)
  1. Leadership,  2. Attila, d. 453. I. Title.
HM141.R6 1989
303.3′4—dc19
                                                88-27739
                                                  CIP

Cover design by Jackie Merri Meyer
Cover illustration by Mark Summers

# Contents

# CONTENTS

# *Author's Note*

**B**eginning as a vague idea some ten years before it commanded my full attention, *Leadership Secrets of Attila the Hun* occupied my early mornings, late nights and weekends for nearly a year. During that period, there were a number of people who provided the encouragement and support necessary to sustain me. I remain indebted to them.

First, I want to express my appreciation to Cheryl, Justin, Jaime and Jeremy, who are not just my family but friends and confidants who provided enduring sanction and assistance throughout the penning of the manuscript and its subsequent revisions. Justin, though just ten years old when this project began, was especially helpful in conceptualizing the book's metaphoric leader, Attila. Cheryl provided penetrating insight into the behavior of leaders from all walks of life. Jaime and Jeremy gave the project the kind of unreserved support that is found only in the innocence of childhood or the magnanimity of adult maturity.

Aniko Myers and Dave Handley provided some excellent background material on Attila—no small feat, since there isn't an abundance of it. Lee Allen, an accomplished military commander and a former army colleague, acted the role of mentor, seeing that I didn't stray too far from the book's primary theme.

In the autumn of 1984, I made several attempts on my own and through a literary agent in Boston to gain the interest of virtually *any* publishing house that would agree to print the book. After being rejected by seventeen publishers for seventeen different reasons, many of them conflicting, I was informed by a second literary agent that my work was one he could not represent. I decided, therefore, to have the good people at Publisher's Press in Salt Lake City print the book at my own expense. My intent became one of providing copies, over time, to people who had an interest in a book that was an audacious break from traditional leadership literature.

Concurrent with these events, David Copus, a prominent Washington, D.C., attorney, read the original manuscript and suggested I send a copy to H. Ross Perot. Soon after the limited first printing, I sent Ross a copy with David's compliments. Ross thought enough of the book to call and discuss it with me. His purchase of seven hundred copies of the first edition, which has since been publicly revealed in Albert Lee's book *Call Me Roger*, inspired me to continue disseminating the book and to also search out possibilities for wider distribution.

Over the course of the next three years, *Leadership Secrets* found its way into the hands of a few thousand Americans, ranging from the most wealthy and influential to the ordinary man on the street. This was a tremendous experience for Cheryl and me. We hadn't advertised the book or provided any information in either of the first two printings as to how one might purchase additional copies, yet would-be readers continued to track us down. We have enjoyed our conversations and correspondence with them. I hope the book has added some value to their lives and thank them for their patronage and words of encouragement. The time during which we distributed *Leadership Secrets* out of a small office in our home—working together with Justin, Jaime and Jeremy to take orders and to package and ship them—is one of the cherished periods we have shared as a family.

In May of 1988, the fortunes of *Leadership Secrets* were dramatically changed by an unexpected plaudit that appeared in the aforementioned *Call Me Roger*, a book that profiled the mismanagement of one of America's largest corporations, General Motors. Author Albert Lee described the contretemps that developed when GM Chairman Roger Smith prohibited his new business associate, Ross Perot, from distributing five hundred copies of *Leadership Secrets* at a dinner attended by the managers of GM's new Saturn division. This was news to me. At the time, I had no idea that Albert Lee's complimentary words would eventually bring the book to the attention of a publisher who had faith in its prospects, Warner Books. Thanks, Al!

The first step in the process was Dr. Hendrie Weisinger's suggestion that I send a copy of *Leadership Secrets* to his literary agent, Richard Pine. A full two months passed before I overcame my fear of yet another rejection and placed a call to Richard. Not surprisingly, he had never heard of my book but said he would take a look at it. Richard, who is a wizard of his trade, placed *Leadership Secrets* with Warner Books in less than two weeks. If this isn't record time in the publishing world, it is in Cedar City, Utah, my hometown, where events occur at a more leisurely pace.

The people at Warner Books have been an absolute delight to work with. I am especially appreciative of my editor, Rick Horgan, who has energetically added his master's touch in polishing my work. Larry Kirshbaum, Warner's president, has enthusiastically directed the overall activities related to this edition from start to finish. They both are, quite simply, the kind of efficacious people lots of us like to be around.

And finally, it has been my privilege to have had the opportunity to be associated with Larry Wiesen over what is nearing a ten-year period at American Express and now Fireman's Fund. He has given me his confidence, trust, timely and wise counsel, personal example of integrity and the latitude that I might learn and achieve many things that would have otherwise quite possibly remained beyond my grasp.

WESS ROBERTS
*Rohnert Park, California*
August 1988

# *Preface*

Attila the Hun is a dubious character upon whom to base a metaphor on leadership. He's been portrayed throughout history as a barbaric, ugly little tyrant whose hordes, in total disregard of accepted principles of conservation, ruthlessly destroyed the beautiful and tranquil countryside, then went on to plunder and pillage numerous cities and villages inhabited by more civilized citizens of European nations.

Void of any characterization as a brilliant leader, a genius civilizer or a compassionate and adept king, the sinister Attila is commonly used as a referent for entertaining satire and serves as a universally agreed upon example of those qualities and attributes dreadfully abhorred in leaders of any generation, organization or cause.

Typically, leadership books are based on the lives

and accomplishments of socially acceptable men and women who have reached the pinnacle of achievement in business, athletics, medicine, entertainment, education, religion or the military. Many of these writings prove to be worthwhile study; in them are valuable lessons for our own leadership development.

It is, however, sometimes a painstaking challenge to extract from these books the essence of the leadership principles contained in them. Even more challenging is the application of the thoughts in these books to our own lives.

Leadership is the privilege to have the responsibility to direct the actions of others in carrying out the purposes of the organization, at varying levels of authority and with accountability for both successful and failed endeavors. It does not constitute a model or system. No model or system of leadership behaviors can anticipate the circumstances, conditions and situations in which the leader must influence the actions of others. An evaluation of leadership principles is an effective base upon which to build other skills that may be important to success in specialized fields.

For this very reason I have chosen Attila as the central figure for this book. His nation has long since vanished, nomadic Huns no longer roam, and he is a most unlikely role model for anyone to emulate. But as I will show, his career presents a compelling and opportune forum for a primer on leadership.

Individually, the Huns were a spirited, perfidious people without common purpose other than to establish their next campsite. Commodities for internal trade didn't exist, so they sought out villages to lay waste to in order to obtain booty that would later be used as barter for food and other supplies necessary for their survival.

There could be no greater leadership challenge than faced the young Attila as he forged these barbaric hordes into a nation of Huns. He was met with the perils, trials and tribulations of masterful deceit not only from the tribes and clans but also from his own brother and uncles. His army marched against more-disciplined, better-trained and -supplied forces.

Few, if any, of his subordinate chieftains shared Attila's dreams of world conquest and a Hunnish homeland. These chieftains had to be convinced, their objections listened to and overcome. Their loyalty was assured out of fear for their lives, awe of Attila's superior logic and greed at the prospect of more bountiful booty than could be obtained by other means.

As a condition of a peace treaty, Attila once secured tribute payments from Theodosius II, emperor of the Eastern Roman Empire. And, perhaps as a tired and aging king, Attila turned his army homeward at the behest of the pope.

Seen in perspectives different from those who wrote his history—much of which must be to some degree apocryphal, if not biased by political preferences— Attila might today be characterized as an entrepreneur, diplomat, social reformer, statesman, civilizer, brilliant field marshal and host of some terrific parties.

But I didn't choose Attila as the metaphoric character of this book for any of these plausible labels or for the purpose of making him a cult hero in a modern age. Rather, Attila's robust life and controversial image as a determined, tough, rugged and intriguing leader —who dared to accomplish difficult tasks and per-

formed challenging feats against "seemingly" insur-
mountable odds —provides a compelling opportunity
for relating leadership fundamentals to a new generation of leaders who have no fear of him and who
might enjoy a novel pedagogic treatment of what can
otherwise be very mundane, unexciting reading.

For those who have little knowledge of who Attila
was and for the purpose of establishing a basis for my
metaphor, I have included a brief history of his life and
legend in the book's introduction. It is essential to point
out to the reader that even the most reputable historians disagree on the size of Attila's army as well as
the total population of the Hunnish confederacy. In
any case, their numbers have most likely been exag-
gerated in both this and other sources. It also seems
reasonable to me that, if noted historians have had
difficulty estimating the size of his army, much of what
else has been recorded is subject to question and in-
terpretation as well. And, while I have attempted to be
objective in establishing Attila as my metaphorical
leader, I have given him and his Huns a slightly more
positive image than can perhaps be found elsewhere.

Each chapter begins with a vignette based on accounts of Attila's life, which serves to establish the referent situation and experience from which he lectures
on various leadership principles to his chieftains and
Huns in campfire settings. Having no direct relationship to familiar headlines and events in this day, these
vignettes provide the reader with an opportunity to
visualize his own situation and prepare himself for
some aphorisms that relate to leadership success in
any age, society, organization or situation.

The aphorisms spoken by Attila in this book have no

basis of authenticity as ever having been said by the King of Huns. They are, rather, ones that I have written based upon my own experiences, research and observations. They have been reviewed and tested by some demanding critics and were only incorporated after having survived considerable scrutiny.

In any work of this nature, one is bound to identify some poignant thoughts that remain after the writing is completed. A few of my finest remnants are provided under theme headings I have collectively coined "Attilaisms." They conclude this leadership primer.

There has been no attempt in this effort to identify any past, present or future leaders as "Attilas." Similarly, no attempt has been made to identify "Attila" organizations. This would only distract from the book's intended message and result in a tireless, moot debate.

There is no magical formula for developing leadership abilities contained in this book. Any extraordinary method for accelerating the acquisition of leadership skills, attitudes and attributes is yet to be discovered. For the time being, as in centuries past, it seems to be the nature of the human being to acquire leadership traits a little at a time—building upon previously learned precepts.

I do not consider the precepts and concepts in this book as the definitive statements of all that is known about leading people. This is, however, a comprehensive, fundamental beginning to an understanding of what we commonly refer to as leadership.

# Introduction:
# In Search of Attila

**R**ambling into history as a nation of mysterious origin, the Huns were a nomadic, multiracial and multilingual conglomeration of tribes. Whether their origin was on the European side of the Urals or from Turkic or Asiatic descent is left largely to rarely transcribed and sometimes confused oral history.

Tied to grazing, purposeless in regard to national goals, the Huns were a nation of loosely bound tribes in perpetual migration. Their warriors rode ahead of the women, who made their homes in skin-covered chariots overflowing with children and the pillage of victory.

Their long migrations were monotonous wanderings stimulated in spirit by endless songs paying reverence to nature. Above these songs rang out a steady cacophony of snorting horses and the cracking of whips.

Clad in the skins and furs of beasts, many of the Huns were characterized by somber, yellowish skin, long arms, large chests and narrow, slanted eyes with a dull glitter of mingled cunning and cruelty. Their warriors had skulls deformed in childhood by a wooden apparatus held fast by leather thongs. The scant beards of the warriors were the result of their cheeks having been seared with hot irons in their youth to retard the growth of facial hair.

They ate raw meat toughened by having been carried in pouches between their thighs or between the flanks of their horses. A portion of their nutrition came from drinking mares' milk.

The weapons of the horde were considered unsophisticated and outlandish even in their own time. Their spirit as warriors was driven by a lust for rapid and sustained movement in pursuit of a paradise of glory filled with pillage and booty.

To the civilized world they were barbarians not far removed from wild animals in both appearance and life-style. The mere presence of the horde often instilled sufficient terror in the people of a region that they abandoned their villages without either resistance or subsequent reprisal.

Out of this perplexing and barbaric past rose one of the most formidable leaders the world has known: Attila, King of Huns.

He was born in a chariot somewhere in the valley of the Danube around the year A.D. 395. Attila was the son of King Mundzuk and could trace his ancestry some thirty-two generations. His was the family that maintained the integrity of the horde's bloodline and distinctly Mongol characteristics.

Learning first to ride on the back of sheep, Attila later developed extraordinary skills of horsemanship. He also became superior in the use of the bow, lance, lariat, sword and whip. These were skills of tradition among his people and dutiful talents for one of noble rank.

He developed a strong sense of pride in his personal strength and a great disdain for the weak. His pride of strength was often publicly displayed on adventurous hunting expeditions, on which he captured wolves and bears in nets, then disemboweled them with a short dagger.

His strong bond and special relationship with his father was prematurely shortened upon King Mundzuk's death while Attila was still a lad. Thereafter, he fell victim to the vicious mercies of his uncles, particularly Rugila, successor to King Mundzuk's throne.

Attila's open criticism of Rugila's policy of entering the horde into the service of foreign nations, whom Attila thought the Huns could easily defeat, changed the course of his youth.

At twelve, Attila was sent as a child hostage to the Roman court of Honorius. In return, Rugila received a youth by the name of Aetius, in fulfillment of the exchange arrangement perpetuated by the Romans.

It was a sinister plan on the part of the empire. On the one hand, the empire taught hostages in its court the customs, traditions and pompous ways of its luxurious life—traits these young hostages would carry back to their own nation, thus serving to extend Roman influence into foreign lands. On the other hand, the youth sent as hostages by the empire greatly enhanced its espionage capabilities.

Attila resisted the propaganda spewed at him by his Roman mentors. He personally rejected everything about them. Though he tried to ignite the spirit of resistance among the other child hostages, his attempts failed. On at least two occasions, Attila tried to escape. Failing to gain freedom, he prowled the palace as if he were a caged animal. His hatred for the empire's policies and practices grew stronger day by day.

Captivity was a time of despair for the young Attila. He had been betrayed by the self-serving Rugila. He was lonely for the Hunnish homeland and customs more familiar to him.

Failing escape, Attila turned his attention to an intense study of the empire while outwardly ceasing to struggle against his hostage status. He studied the Romans' internal and foreign policies. He often secretly observed them in diplomatic conference with foreign ministers. He studied the empire's military, observing its strengths and vulnerabilities. He learned about leadership, protocol and other essentials suited to future rulers and diplomats from skilled Romans.

It was in the Roman court that Attila conceived his strategy to rule the world. His plan was methodical, extraordinarily precise. It was not the plan of a blundering half-wit.

While Attila was in the court of Honorius, Aetius, his lifelong nemesis, was serving similar time in the court of King Rugila.

Aetius was born into the family of Gaudentius, son of a German of Pannonia, who bore the titles "Master of the Horse" and "Count of Africa." His relationship with his father was, as was Attila's with his, abbreviated by his father's death during a revolt of his own soldiers in Gaul.

During his period as a child hostage, Aetius developed a trusted relationship with King Rugila and other Hunnish nobles. Likewise, he became a scholar of the Huns—learning their customs, traditions and motives. They schooled him in the mastery of their weapons, taught him to hunt and to ride, providing the foundation from which Aetius would later deal with Attila at the Battle of Châlons.

On Attila's return to the valley of the Danube, the tribes remained independent from political or military control by a central throne.

Attila began his rise to power by renewing and developing relationships with tribal chieftains. Much of this familiarization came through Attila's many hunting expeditions throughout the Hunnish territories. He gained the loyalty of these chieftains through emotional appeal, arousing their warrior instincts and whetting their appetites for easily gained glory and pillage.

How Attila became king over the tribe in the valley of the Danube is said, by historical accounts, to be the result of his brother Bleda's death during a hunt. A more romantic legend among the Huns gives his rise another origin.

According to this legend, on the death of Bleda, tribal leaders, gathered in mourning, argued over who would become their king. During this council a lad reported a flaming sword had just appeared in the midst of a nearby meadow. Following the lad to the meadow, the tribal chieftains watched in awe as the flaming sword jumped into Attila's outstretched hand. The sword's craftsmanship was of such quality it was assumed to have been made by a deity. It was an omen, "the Sword of God." Surely it was sent to them to end this quarrel and to confirm Attila as their king.

Once he became king over the royal tribe, Attila began his unification of the other fiercely independent tribes into a Hunnish nation.

He is said to have spent days in front of his tent in conference with tribal chieftains to confirm their loyalties to his unification plan. Attila summarily executed rebellious chieftains. The fear of resistance to him became so manifest that one aging chieftain excused himself from a personal audience with King Attila by saying, "My eyes, too weak to behold the sun, could assuredly not look upon the brilliance of the conqueror." This artful flattery was accepted by Attila without objection.

Although he leveraged its power, he was not seduced by the trappings of his new office. Drinking and eating from implements made of wood, Attila sat on a wooden throne in a wooden palace. His dress showed none of the elegance of the Roman rulers. Rather, he wore a coat of black fur and a black leather cap pulled down over his eyes.

Attila was held in high regard by the horde. His entry into their camps was something to behold. Women, children and warriors lined his path shouting praises to him. Women presented food to him as he rode by them. Attila accepted these gestures with dignity, hastily eating the food while still remaining on the back of his gallant black charger, Villam.

His rule as King of Huns was marked by swift yet considerate justice. He did not act in haste. He gave the Huns a national goal—to bring under their control the Germanic and Slavic nations, to conquer Rome and Constantinople, to march against all of Asia, then on to Africa. Thus, the Huns would reign over all the lands to the north, south, east and west. Indeed, Attila would rule the world.

Attila's plan was ambitious, fired by boyhood dreams, shaped by those images formed in his youth. He aimed to realize it step by step. His method was tempered by patience and unrelenting tenacity born of Asiatic virtues and by the political insight mastered by one who listens and watches while he waits for the precise moment to act.

The conquests of the Huns under his rule are legendary. Attila was skillful in the execution of his plan. His army, by many estimates to have consisted of as many as 700,000 warriors, was a conglomeration of barbarians. Yet it became single in purpose, well disciplined and filled with esprit de corps.

Even though the momentum of the Huns proceeded with difficulty at times, victory was often theirs without local resistance. Villages were, at times, abandoned upon hearing of the Hunnish army's approach. Yet this forward movement of the Huns was to be abruptly frustrated by Aetius, the lifelong rival of their ruler.

In A.D. 451, on the Catalaunian Plains near Châlons, in the ruins of an ancient Roman camp, the Huns massed their chariots in preparation for battle. The Romans were led into the conflict that would ensue by Aetius. The Huns were under Attila's personal command.

Using tactics gained from his experience among the Huns, Aetius neutralized the advantage of the Hunnish army's bows and cavalry by engaging them in hand-

to-hand combat. The bronze helmets and body armament of the Roman soldiers shielded them from the
stone axes of the barbarians, who were unskilled in
infantry tactics. The swords of the Romans prevailed
over the lariats and long lances of the Huns. The battle
was savage, neither side took prisoners, and few of the
wounded survived. It is believed that by nightfall, between 162,000 and 300,000 Hunnish warriors lay dead
on the Catalaunian Plains.

Realizing the futility of this battle's continuance, Attila ordered a retreat, leaving the Romans somewhat
astonished to see the Hunnish horde's backside in Attila's first, and only, defeat. Something in Attila's plan
had gone wrong and, for a moment in time, his confidence, unrelenting energy and will seemed to desert
him. His optimistic desire to conquer the world dwindled before him in tormenting defeat.

Returning his battered army to the familiar valley of
the Danube, Attila turned his energy toward military
science and the necessary changes to set out once again
in his conquest of the world. A reorganization of his
army sufficient to implement the radical change necessary to overcome the tactics of his adversary Aetius
would not be without profound alterations in the customs held for generation upon generation by the Huns.

Leather armor with borders of metal plates replaced
the fur garments of his army. The Huns' capital city,
Etzelburg, was fortified to withstand long sieges. Their
nomadic life-style was laid aside; they were no longer
unstable and wandering—they had a homeland and
had become deeply rooted in its soil, had even become
civilized. Catapults were prepared. Warriors were drilled
in infantry tactics—learning to maneuver on foot, their

protection no longer being the safety provided by accuracy with the bow but in the use of long shields.

Circumstances brought about by developing allegiances between the Persians and the Romans prematurely halted Attila's plans to completely restructure the Hunnish army. Immediate action was necessary to prevent the consequences of this alliance. Attila gathered his tribal chieftains and, in a few words, laid out their route of march and order of battle.

The return of the Huns to battle was not perceived by many Romans as any great peril to their safety. They had not been witness to the Hunnish army's ability to savagely devastate what lay before them. They were shortly to become more familiar with the fury of the barbaric swarm.

After a swift and unobstructed entry into Italy, the Huns laid siege to Aquileia, a bastion accustomed to invasions. Soon the Aquileians saw the Huns not as blundering savages but as a well-equipped and -disciplined army, skillful in the execution of military movements.

The siege was long, rations became scarce, and Hunnish morale threatened to fade. But when the now-disciplined warriors attacked upon the sighting of a good omen—that of a stork and its brood leaving the city's towers—victory was instant! The walls crumbled, and the city was set in flames.

The horde was allowed time to ransack, and then they set off in a fresh fighting spirit, renewed by this major triumph. Aquileian survivors told the empire of Attila's vast army, now advancing ferociously, methodically, on Rome. The empire was exasperated! It now feared this seemingly unstoppable force.

As they could no longer rely on the genius of the great General Aetius, who had long since fallen from grace, the Roman leaders were at a loss. At first they thought of offering gold for ransom, but decided this would not satisfy a horde that could just as easily add all of Italy's treasure to the booty that already overflowed their chariots.

In desperation, the Emperor Valentinian thought of another tactic. Why not offer Honoria, his sister, to Attila as a wife? Had this not even been promised in a treaty of long ago? This plan was put aside when it was suggested that since there had been no earlier demand by Attila for the hand of Honoria, perhaps the King of Huns was content with his more than 300 wives.

Lacking any suitable alternative, and without consulting Aetius, Valentinian sent Pope Leo I to negotiate with Attila. The emperor hoped that perhaps through respect for the clergy, the Scourge of God would show mercy as he had one year earlier in Gaul when he acceded to Bishop Lupus' request and spared the city of Troyes.

What transpired between the frail pope and the King of Huns remains a mystery. But, after their meeting, Attila turned his army northward, sparing Rome, and returned to his homeland, avoiding further battle.

Trouble was brewing for Attila in the valley of the Danube. His six favored sons were impatient at not having received their own kingdoms as promised earlier by their father. They were frustrated that he had returned without conquering lands for them.

Perhaps it was his advancing age that tempered his ambitions of world conquest. Possibly it was Attila's diminishing self-confidence, or a personal calming of his ambitions in the satisfaction in having willingly spared Rome. World conquest was no longer an unfulfilled need. The warrior in him was now turning more toward diplomacy. He resumed negotiations with the Romans. These actions, unfamiliar during his rule, made it necessary for disciplinary reasons that Attila reconfirm himself as King of Huns. Again, as in earlier years, he executed chieftains who rebelled against him.

The beautiful young daughter of one such rebel chieftain implored Attila to spare her father, who was, nevertheless, executed. Attila was, however, touched by her beauty and decided to take the girl, Ildico, as his wife. The marriage was considered to be a good omen by the Huns—Attila would forget his old age, his disappointments and troubles and return to his pursuit of world conquest with new vigor. Thus, his sons would be given territories over which they could rule.

After a convivial wedding ceremony, which is still held in legendary awe, the royal couple retired to their nuptial chamber. On the following day, in the midst of an uncustomary silence from their king, the unanswered door of the nuptial chamber was smashed open by his warriors. There lying naked on a white fur was Attila, dead, his body motionless in a pool of blood!

Some say his bride slew him to revenge the death of her father; however, no wounds were discovered. Some say perhaps his sons, impatient with their father, killed him. The romantic and legendary version of Attila's death is that he died from natural causes—hemorrhage brought on by the excessive festiveness of his wedding.

Attila's burial was as colorful as his wedding had been. In a great and majestic ceremony, he was buried beneath the Tisza River.

Western history, in which Attila is described as cruel and inordinately ruthless, holds no reverence for him. That has laid the foundation for innuendoes and puns regarding his character and mannerisms. Similar traits manifested by notorious leaders in all subsequent generations were considered cold-blooded and evil.

He has been scorned by authors as prominent as Dante in *The Divine Comedy, Inferno, Canto XII*, in which he wrote, "There Heaven's stern justice lays chastising hand on Attila, who was the scourge of earth."

In his fictitious final confession to the North Koreans, the commander of the USS *Pueblo*, Lloyd Bucher, appealed to his captors "to forgive our dastardly deeds unmatched since Attila." Later, Commander Bucher swore to the enemy that his account of the *Pueblo*'s actions was ". . . true on the sacred honor of the Great Speckled Bird." Again, Attila bore the brunt of a timely use of the pen.

Yet, Attila is proudly remembered by many of his remnant people, the Hungarians. Perhaps the German Nibelungen-Lied said it best for them when he wrote, "There was a mighty king in the land of the Huns whose goodness and wisdom had no equal."

Attila is an example of the type of leader who is never satisfied—preferring to take the initiative, acting rather than doing nothing.

Attila was less savage than the Romans, who cast thousands of Christians to wild animals for mere entertainment. In comparison, he was less cruel than Ivan the Terrible, Cortés or Pizarro. In his sparing of Rome, he showed more mercy than did Genserich, Belizar, the Norsemen, the Germans and the Spanish mercenaries, who all pillaged it without regard.

Attila's legacy is generally unfamiliar to us in the Western World. We are naive about his historical importance as a genius civilizer, his open-mindedness and richness of views, in all of which he far exceeded Alexander the Great or Caesar.

The controversy surrounding Attila will perhaps never be resolved, but his "leadership secrets" present insightful opportunity to learn, by way of metaphor, age-old characteristics, values and principles that separate those who lead from those who follow.

After all, he became Attila, King of Huns!

# 1

# *In the Roman Court: "Leadership Qualities"*

**C**leverly influencing other nations from Rome, the empire used a child-hostage exchange arrangement to broaden control over countries it sought to seduce into its servitude. Simply stated, the empire sent one of its own to a foreign nation and those nations reciprocated by sending one of their own sons to live and learn in the Roman courts.

This cunning approach was a masterful exercise in subversive diplomacy. The honored countries were infiltrated at their highest levels by the youthful spies for the empire. Once in the foreign courts, the young Romans reported vital information back to the empire while gaining personal knowledge of the customs, courtesies and traditions of their hosts. This two-edged strategy also gave the empire the opportunity to tutor the hostages sent to its court. Teaching them the luxuries of life served to influence the politics and culture of less-civilized and subservient nations when the matured hostages returned to their native land.

Apparently once the favored nephew of King Rugila, Attila diminished his standing with the Hunnish throne by his constant harsh criticism of policies that placed the horde in the service of the empire and other foreign nations. It became convenient for Rugila to use the Roman practice to rid himself of his chief critic.

Not yet in his teens, Attila was sent to the Roman court of Honorius. There, thought Rugila, the tutelage of the empire would surely develop characteristics in Attila that would make him a more compatible member of the Huns' royal family.

Attila personally rejected the fancy robes, pompous hairstyles, rich foods and perfumed quarters offered to him as a hostage, though such trappings intrigued his unsophisticated comrades. Attila attempted, but was unable, to ignite their spirit to resist this and other beguiling propaganda imposed by the empire. After failing to escape, Attila resolved to use passive resistance and to adapt to his temporary circumstances.

In the Roman court, he watched and listened. With each passing day he became more and more determined to rid the world of Roman and mysterious Christian influences. Attila was an extraordinary student of the internal and foreign policies of the empire. He grew in his awareness of their armies, weapons, order of battle and their lack of a strong navy. Attila used this period to spy on visiting ministers, to seek out the intrigues of the empire and to learn about policy making and diplomacy.

Life in the Roman court was a tremendous hardship

for Attila. He was lonely for his people, for his family, and yearned to free them from the service of a strange and foreign nation that the Huns, once united, could surely defeat.

The boy who was sent as a hostage to the court of Honorius profited from his Asiatic virtue of patience. His attitude was one of stoicism and certitude. He learned that pushing events to happen before their time was less important than their ultimate achievement. He, therefore, set out to develop the personal abilities that would ensure his success at the time that he would actively pursue his reign as King of Huns.

# ATTILA ON:
## "LEADERSHIP QUALITIES"

As we gather in this counsel, I, Attila, have prepared my innermost thoughts regarding leadership qualities. These thoughts I give you so you and your subordinates might be better prepared to lead the Huns.

It is essential to the Hunnish nation that we have in our service leaders at every level who possess the skills, abilities and attitudes that will enable them to successfully carry out the responsibilities incumbent to their office.

There is no quick way to develop leaders. Huns must learn throughout their lives—never ceasing as students, never being above gaining new insights or studying innovative procedures or methods—whatever the source.

Our leaders must learn early in their service certain

basic qualities and have opportunities to mature in them.

We must teach these qualities to our young warriors, if they are to develop into able chieftains. Basic instruction in horsemanship, with the lariat, bow and lance, is sufficient for our warriors but not for those who lead them.

In order to skillfully lead our nation, we must have chieftains who possess, among others, the following essential qualities, which through experience become mastered skills:

- **LOYALTY**—Above all things, a Hun must be loyal. Disagreement is not necessarily disloyalty. A Hun who, in the best interest of the tribe, disagrees, should be listened to. On the other hand, a Hun who actively participates in or encourages actions that are counter to the good of the tribe is disloyal. These Huns, whether warrior or chieftain, must be expeditiously removed. Their ability to influence and discourage loyal Huns is a contagious disease. In cases where disloyal actions and attitudes cannot be changed, harsh action must be taken to rid ourselves of those among us who see no value in and subvert our cause.

- **COURAGE**—Chieftains who lead our Huns must have courage. They must be fearless and have the fortitude to carry out assignments given them—the gallantry to accept the risks of leadership. They must not balk at the sight of obstacles, nor must they become bewildered when in the presence of adversity. The role of a chieftain has inherent periods of loneliness, despair, ridicule and rejection. Chieftains must be long-suffering in their duties—they must have the courage to act with confidence and to excel in times of uncertainty or danger as well as in times of prosperity.

■ **DESIRE**—Few Huns will sustain themselves as chieftains without strong personal desire—an inherent commitment to influencing people, processes and outcomes. Weak is the chieftain who does not want to be one. We must be careful to avoid placing capable warriors into positions of leadership that they have no desire to fulfill.

■ **EMOTIONAL STAMINA**—Each succeedingly higher level of leadership places increasing demands on the emotions of chieftains. We must ensure that our leaders at every level have the stamina to recover rapidly from disappointment—to bounce back from discouragement, to carry out the responsibilities of their office without becoming distorted in their views—without losing clear perspective, as well as the emotional strength to persist in the face of seemingly difficult circumstances.

■ **PHYSICAL STAMINA**—Huns must have chieftains who can endure the physical demands of their leadership duties. Chieftains must nurture their bodies with the basic, healthful staples. Chieftains cannot lead from their bedside. They lack energy when filled with too much food or drink. The distorting potions of the Romans only confuse minds. A body not properly used becomes abused. A healthy body supports a healthy mind. Our chieftains must be strong in body in order to lead the charge.

■ **EMPATHY**—Chieftains must develop empathy—an appreciation for and an understanding of the values of others, a sensitivity for other cultures, beliefs and traditions. However, empathy must not be confused with sympathy, which may result in unwise consolation in times when, above all other things, the good of the tribe or nation must be pursued with adroit diplomacy or battlefield action.

■ **DECISIVENESS**—Young chieftains must learn to be decisive, knowing when to act and when not to act, taking into account all facts bearing on the situation and then responsibly carrying out their leadership role. Vacillation and procrastination confuse and discourage subordinates, peers and superiors and serve the enemy well.

■ **ANTICIPATION**—Learning by observation and through instincts sharpened by tested experience, our chieftains must anticipate thoughts, actions and consequences. Anticipation bears a level of risk that is willingly accepted by a chieftain who will excel when others turn to the comfort of personal security.

■ **TIMING**—Essential to all acts of leadership is the timing of recommendations and actions. There is no magic formula for developing a sense of timing. One often gains this leadership skill by applying the lessons learned through failure. Knowing whom you are dealing with, their motives, characters, priorities and ambitions are critical elements even when seeking approval of the simplest recommendation.

■ **COMPETITIVENESS**—An essential quality of leadership is an intrinsic desire to win. It is not necessary to win all the time; however, it is necessary to win the important contests. Chieftains must understand that the competition inside and outside our nation is strong and not to be taken lightly. A sense of competitive anger drives those who win on the battlefield, in negotiations and in situations of internal strife. A leader without a sense of competitiveness is weak and easily overcome by the slightest challenge.

- **SELF-CONFIDENCE**—Proper training and experience develops in chieftains a personal feeling of assurance with which to meet the inherent challenges of leadership. Those who portray a lack of self-confidence in their abilities to carry out leadership assignments give signs to their subordinates, peers and superiors that these duties are beyond their capabilities. They become, therefore, weak leaders and useless chieftains.

- **ACCOUNTABILITY**—Learning to account for personal actions and those of subordinates is fundamental to leadership. Chieftains must never heap praise or lay blame on others for what they themselves achieve or fail to accomplish, no matter how glorious or grave the consequences.

- **RESPONSIBILITY**—Leaders are only necessary when someone is to be responsible to see that actions are carried out and directions followed. No king, chieftain or subordinate leader should ever be allowed to serve who will not accept full responsibility for his actions.

- **CREDIBILITY**—Chieftains must be credible. Their

words and actions must be believable to both friend and foe. They must be trusted to have the intelligence and integrity to provide correct information. Leaders lacking in credibility will not gain proper influence and are to be hastily removed from positions of responsibility, for they cannot be trusted.

■ **TENACITY**—The quality of unyielding drive to accomplish assignments is a desirable and essential quality of leadership. The weak persist only when things go their way. The strong persist and pursue through discouragement, deception and even personal abandonment. Pertinacity is often the key to achieving difficult assignments or meeting challenging goals.

■ **DEPENDABILITY**—If a chieftain cannot be depended upon in all situations to carry out his roles and responsibilities, relieve him of them. A king cannot observe each and every action of his subordinate chieftains; therefore, he must depend upon them to get things done. Young chieftains should understand that Huns serving above and below them in the tribe and nation are counting on their ability to lead, and they should be proud of being entrusted with such responsibility.

■ **STEWARDSHIP**—Our leaders must have the essential quality of stewardship, a caretaker quality. They must serve in a manner that encourages confidence, trust and loyalty. Subordinates are not to be abused; they are to be guided, developed and rewarded for their performance. Punishment is to be reserved as a consequence of last resort and sparingly applied only when all other attempts have failed to encourage the rebellious to comply. Without a flock there can be no shepherd. Without an army there can be no battle captains. Without subordinates there can be no leaders. Leaders are, therefore, caretakers of the interests and well-being of those and the purposes they serve.

Those of you who are overly ambitious may attempt to acquire these qualities over a short period. As I, Attila, have found in my own life, these qualities of leadership simply take time, learning and experience to develop. There are few who will find shortcuts. There are simply rare opportunities to accelerate competence, and without paying the price, no matter how great or small, none will become prepared to lead others.

Learn these leadership qualities well. Teach them to the Huns. Only then will we expand our ability to lead our vast nation in pursuit of world conquest.

# 2

# The Lust for Leadership: "You've Got to Want to Be in Charge"

On the death of his father, Mundzuk, Attila came under the guidance and care of his uncle Rugila. Soon after his reign as king began, Rugila—enticed by the immediacy of reward, deceived by sinister diplomacy, and having no awareness of the terror inspired in other nations by his tribes—entered the horde into the service of the empire.

Even in his youth, Attila believed in the noble past and legends of his ancestry. They were a strong and powerful people, not to be subjected to slave rule or indentured service.

Though the Huns had roamed the vast regions of Europe and portions of Asia and Africa, their leaders, Attila's noble progenitors, had never let their tribes perform unnecessary service for strangers. Rather, they had persisted in their search for a peaceful place in which they would be free to pursue a pastoral existence.

Attila became an outspoken critic of King Rugila and his policies, for Rugila's motives and decisions were perceived by the young prince as contrary to the strengths, purposes and good of the Hunnish people. Attila's criticism diminished his favor with Rugila, who perceived the lad as a threat to the security of his noble position and shipped the child off to the Roman court early in his life. Attila began to develop a hatred for ignoble rule and a lust to lead those who could help him right the situation.

While a hostage, Attila attempted to unite other "barbarians" in rejecting the intrigues of the empire. They were not to fall victim and become servants of the empire! They must retain their own identities! Though his efforts to unite them failed, his determination to lead waxed with each passing day.

Attila turned his anger, distaste and contempt for the empire into an energetic study to learn the ways of leadership and diplomacy. His mind was fueled by the fires burning deep in his heart to unite the Huns and conquer the Romans.

Instead of immediately attempting to gain control on his return to his homeland, Attila was patient, his every step planned. He knew his leadership knowledge and abilities to influence must mature no matter how driven his desires to take charge. Attila traveled and hunted, using the time to focus his ambition into a plan that would succeed.

When the moment came, Attila was ready! He took charge! He was prepared in every way to face the challenges and opposition he would encounter as king. He would not be discouraged! He would not deviate from his objective! He was ready to take risks, ready to cause the Huns to excel through unity of action. His dogged perseverance and lust to assume a position of considerable responsibility had held—his destiny had arrived! Attila had become King of Huns.

## ATTILA ON: "YOU'VE GOT TO WANT TO BE IN CHARGE"

There is little more unsettling to Huns than being under the command of a king or chieftain who shows a lack of commitment in his responsibility as a leader.

Too often, the leadership of many nations falls to princes who lack the ambition, courage and capabilities to reign as leaders. Such disinterest, cowardice and incompetence is manifested in various actions that discourage and bewilder subordinates, thus strengthening the enemy.

It is the responsibility of all Huns to choose and follow only those chieftains who demonstrate a desire to lead. Such leaders will be of no composite character. They will be as different from one another as one Hun is different from another. They will not be laden with all human virtues, nor will they possess a flawless character.

Committed leaders, those with a lust for leadership, a willingness to serve, will, however, be distinguishable by their wisdom, sincerity, benevolence, authority and courage. They will have a human quality and a strong commitment to their cause and to that of those they serve.

Huns who aspire to become chieftains often do not have such motives from the time they leave the comfort of the chariot. Now perhaps you Huns would ask of me, "How, Attila, might I know if I possess sufficient desire to be a chieftain?" To those who wish my counsel, I offer these thoughts:

■ Above all other traits, one who desires to lead must possess an intrinsic desire to achieve substantial personal recognition and be willing to earn it in all fairness.

■ You must have resilience to overcome personal misfortunes, discouragement, rejection and disappointment.

■ You must have the courage, creativity and stamina to focus on accomplishing your responsibilities through the directed, delegated efforts of subordinates.

■ You must recognize and accept that your greatness will be made possible through the extremes of your personality—the very extremes that sometimes make for campfire satire and legendary stories.

■ You must not let your desire to lead take the form of overeagerness. This would cause failure for many. You must be willing to temper your lust to lead with preparation, experience and opportunity.

■ You must remember that success in your office will depend largely upon your sustained willingness to work hard. Sweat rules over inspiration!

- You must be committed to persevere even in the face of opposition and challenge.

- You must be determined to apply massive common sense in solving complex problems.

- You must not be threatened by capable contemporaries or subordinates. Rather, you must be wise in selecting capable captains to achieve those things a chieftain can attain only through strong subordinates.

- You must be willing to make unrecognized and thankless personal sacrifice for those you serve and those you lead. This sacrifice may take the form of absence from a tribal hunt, spending extraordinary energies and patience to develop subordinates and tending to the needs of these subordinates at times when your own needs go unfulfilled. You must be willing to bypass a festival in your own camp if a situation in another camp requires your presence and attention.

- You must have a passion to succeed—a passion that drives you to prepare yourself and your Huns to excel.

- You must be willing to learn, to listen and to grow in your awareness and abilities to perform the duties of your office. This is not often accomplished without tremendous effort and sacrifice of other interests.

- You must be willing to remain your natural self and

not take on an aura of false pride in your countenance.

■ You must be willing to accept the simple fact that you have flaws and will need to work every day to become a better chieftain than you were yesterday.

I leave you with the admonition to never accept an office of leadership for which you are not willing to pay the tribute necessary to successfully fulfill its obligations.

# 3

# *Becoming a Hun: "Customs"*

The Huns were a collection of fiercely independent multiracial and multilingual tribes, a people without recognizable physical characteristics, with no observable religion but talented in military and political matters and marked by a common thread of mercurial instability and emotional heroism. Yet they were tempered by their nomadic qualities, which for centuries led them on constant migrations in search of a peaceful, pastoral existence.

The Huns had a certain magical magnetism that affected both friend and foe. They could assimilate foreigners into their tribes as well as they could integrate themselves into foreign nations. They were a unique people of a complex culture, the synthesis of all they'd encountered. Although the Huns were feared, thousands of foreigners joined them and even died for their cause. They possessed a certain commonality of national character that often seemed to be of a contrasting nature.

Known for their respect for women, elders and ancestors, the Huns had a conservative moral philosophy. They rejected secular or religious doctrines and practices that made man subordinate to abstract concepts of a philosophical, political or social nature. Their guilelessness and naive faith in human goodness frequently caused them to fall prey to the intricacies of more skilled practitioners of diplomacy.

Their songs were simple, endless tales of nostalgic utterances filled with love for nature. In all tribes, one could find a strong interest in romantic history and also applied humor filled with political satire.

Huns believed strongly in miracles, held beautiful but useless ideals and were a people of optimism and flexibility. Their love of the hunt was well-established in their tradition. It was, perhaps, the Huns who began the custom of the "stag party."

In all, they were a nation with basic attitudes toward life and mankind, yet their love of freedom, excessive pride and volatile tempers often caused them to reject both military and political discipline.

The Huns were a constituency of vast differences who, nevertheless, held common virtues, and it was perhaps their strong sense of honor and loyalty, paired with Attila's intense personal appeal, that united them into a nation that for a short time was a powerful military and diplomatic force.

# ATTILA ON: "CUSTOMS"

All who are Huns and those who seek to become one of us must learn, adapt and adhere to our customs. If they are not Huns, then we must suspect them to be Romans or to be allies of the empire; therefore, we must treat them with caution.

It is not essential that a Hun compromise those characteristics that make him a unique warrior. Every Hun, however, must be willing to conform to those things that distinguish us as a nation of strong, unified tribes. We must be single in purpose, yet individuality that does not distract from the tribe or nation must be preserved.

What is good for the Hun must be good for the tribe and nation. Conversely, what is good for the tribe and nation must be good for the Hun; otherwise, he will desert to the Romans.

When we prescribe dress for battle, celebration, ceremony or other occasions, Huns will see to it that they wear that which is customary.

When we establish Hunnish methods, they must be taught to our young so they will know what is expected of them in every situation. If Huns do not learn the rules, their chieftains cannot expect them to be followed.

Our songs and dances must be unique in the celebration of our noble heritage. We must not introduce into them contaminants that may cause our heritage to become confused.

Our approach toward exacting tribute and loyalties from those we have chosen as the opposition must continue to use and increase the strength of the nation. Only when we fail to recognize our power and influence over the adversary have they set us back.

We must modify our customs when the situation warrants, if such an alteration will strengthen our position. We cannot, however, distill those customs that remain key to the success of the Hunnish nation. We cannot permit strong chieftains or groups of young Huns to attempt the founding of customs that serve only their purpose. Customs are of nations, not of individuals.

Being a Hun requires dedication and devotion to the cause of our nation. Following our customs is a tribute to our heritage—and to our present and future.

Huns are required to make oaths of lasting obligation to the nation. We, in turn, as leaders, must ensure that we have customs—strong traditions—worthy of such a lasting conviction and must welcome into our tribes and nation all who adhere to those principles and ways we value now and forever.

To a nation of such robust and independent heritage, I, Attila, give counsel as to those things we admonish all to honor as our customs:

- It is the custom of all Huns to hold strong to personal and national honor. This is a cardinal virtue. One's word must prevail over all other considerations, including political expediency.

- We must value the capable Hun, whether of lowly or of noble birth. We must appoint our chieftains from among those most qualified to lead, regardless of ancestry.

- We must not retaliate against the innocent, use unscrupulous tactics or kill unsuspecting or trapped enemies. We must be fierce in the eyes of all we seek to influence, yet the use of unnecessary terror is ignoble.

■ A nation of one ancestry and race is weak. We must hold strong our custom of welcoming all foreigners who seek to join our cause, treating them with dignity and respect and teaching them our language and customs.

■ Our accepted differences and diversities must be pooled into a common purpose worthy of our efforts as tribes and as a nation.

■ Our racial, cultural, moral and social concepts, inherited from our ancestors of Asia and Europe, must be recognized and honored by all, through respect for our fellow man, his faculties and well-being.

■ We must never build pyramids in our own honor. While we hold strong the custom of individual and national pride, we must not fall victim to pompous, self-serving practices that weaken the fiber of our vitality and appeal to those we serve.

■ We must hold fast to our custom of high ideals and optimism—never being discouraged by those who would seek to gain personal or national advantage over us.

■ Our songs, dances, games, jests and celebrations must always remain steadfast as propitious opportunity to renew our allegiance and identity as Huns.

You chieftains have the responsibility to continue to teach and practice the customs that make our diverse people and tribes a strong and powerful Hunnish nation, lest they falter for lack of an identity.

# Peace in the Camp: "Morale and Discipline"

The camps of the Huns enjoyed a spirited life with pronounced fluctuations in joy and sorrow. Victory brought about joy, sounds of celebration and ephemeral feelings of security. The death of warriors, periods of diminished supplies and tribal struggles brought on sorrow and despair.

Hunnish morale and discipline was either very high or very low. Seldom, if ever, was theirs a life of status quo. Ambitious Huns could undermine the rule of weak chieftains and throw the camp into confusion. The absence of a national cause contributed to the mixed patterns of morale and discipline.

The Huns' ways were more attuned to an uncertain life, to a morale that was fired by battle, booty or caravaning to a new home. They were in fact disciplined only by the bounds of nature and the whims of fortune and charged with the morale of a people holding tenaciously to optimistic determination.

Attila's task as King of Huns was to instill a new sense of morale and discipline that would provide unity in and among the barbaric tribes. Their greater destiny was served only by setting aside past individual customs as smaller, independent, undisciplined bands of nomads. Peace in the camps would only result from a new spirit of nationalism. Attila's was not a simple chore!

## ATTILA ON: "MORALE AND DISCIPLINE"

The traditions of our nomadic life have given little concern to our morale and discipline as a nation.

We have had passing moments of unity among our tribes, but this unity has been set aside when tribal loyalties have been purchased by foreign nations.

Our people need the constancy of knowing what it means to be a Hun. Their spirit as Huns has been betrayed each time they've been subjected to an alliance with a nation we could surely conquer.

Morale and discipline as Huns is utmost if we are to pass the tests imposed upon us as a unified nation.

I have called you together at this time to teach you the ways of morale and discipline. Through them we may have peace in our camps.

Listen and learn from my counsel.

■ Morale and discipline are central to unity.

■ The conclusive test of the morale of your Huns is

the disciplined manner in which they bear the burdens of trial.

- Discipline is not suppression. It is the teaching of correct ways expected of Huns.

- Without discipline, Huns cannot behave with common action.

- Morale is the spirit by which Huns submit their services to the tribe. It is not uncontrolled celebration and romping around the campfire.

- Discipline is not always welcomed by Huns.

- Chieftains must work hard to establish discipline and morale, then to maintain them within the tribe.

- Discipline does not mean a loss of individuality.

- Discipline never allows deviation from order or from principles we hold important among our tribes or nation.

- Morale results from pride in being a Hun. Discipline brings about morale.

- Chieftains never condone a lack of either morale or discipline. They plan for morale and discipline! They cause it to happen!

- Discipline builds the inner confidence of our Huns. Thus, discipline builds morale.

- Huns seek discipline in their lives. They more willingly follow chieftains who are themselves disciplined.

- Lack of morale and discipline is the most contagious and destructive disease that can ever enter your camp.

- Morale and discipline is largely what chieftains make of it.

- Wise chieftains cause Huns to be tested in their discipline through a successive scheme of opportunities in which their physical and emotional stamina is tried. However, chieftains should never test Huns beyond reasonable capacity.

- Discipline should be expected only at those levels of order and conformity that serve the good of the tribe or nation. Demanding more than is required is an abuse of power and will give rise to rebellion within the tribe.

- Wise chieftains realize that unduly harsh or unnecessarily lax discipline will undo the morale of their Huns.

Peace and harmony in your camps will come from reasonable expectation of disciplined action and purpose. Morale will accompany such reasonable exacting of discipline. There is no simple pattern by which morale and discipline can be attained. These critical secrets to your success as leaders are rather an awareness—an attitude—by which you carry out the charge of your office.

The morale and discipline attained in your camps bears its fruits of reward when exploiting your strengths on the battlefield or in diplomatic encounters.

Now, having the benefit of my counsel, go forth to your camps and instill, even demand, new purpose of unity, new pride in being a Hun. The loyalty, dedication and spirit of your Huns will instill in all our camps confidence, comfort and peace, without which we will continue to have widespread discontent and will return to a life of aimless wandering.

# 5

# The Fury of Internal Battles: "Cunning in the Tribes"

**T**he Huns, long divided into independent tribes, obeyed the precepts of nomadic life. They were still not a nation but small tribes bound together solely by their customs.

As a political matter, the king who reigned on the banks of the Danube held no authority over the Huns of Asia or Russia. Chieftains ruled their subject tribes as they wished, pillaged on their own accord and migrated whenever resources had become exhausted. Never did they trouble to plan what their next destination might be.

Intermarriages with conquered races were numerous. Without the powerful forces of unification, the Huns would have slowly been consumed into the medley of European races.

Attila, son of Mundzuk and a descendant of the ancient imperial family extending back thirty-two generations to Cham, faced little opposition so long as he did not seek to force his authority over the chieftains not directly subject to him.

Thus it happened that the Huns were often under orders of different nations. Their chieftains often sold themselves and their warriors as dearly as possible, showing no reluctance to fight against even men of their own race.

No national sentiment could exist in a people so broken up, no concerted action was possible when everyone played his own hand. Uprooted, driven hither and thither by caprice or need, the Huns wasted their strength in battles from which they gained no profit.

Attila comprehended that, once knit together and strengthened by such nations as were associated with them, the Huns could easily become a mighty power. At a time when the Huns had nothing to fear either from Rome or Constantinople, he devoted himself to the task of forging the instrument necessary for the conquest of the world—a Hunnish army destined to become invincible.

But first the army had to be assembled and the independent tribes consolidated, and in these labors there would be no lack of obstacles. The first presented themselves in his own family.

# ATTILA ON:
## "CUNNING IN THE TRIBES"

The Hunnish nation is comprised not only of those who have long ridden on our many journeys but of all who seek to join us in our romantic ventures as well. To obtain our full potential as rulers of the world, we must openly welcome into our tribes all who seek the nature and fulfillment that comes with being a Hun. The worth of a Hun is not determined by tenure. A Hun's value rests solely upon his demonstrated desire to support, under all circumstances, those goals we seek as a nation of unified tribes.

Among our tribes we have suffered ills brought on by chieftains and Huns who prefer their own ambitions to those of the nation. These are clearly those who, openly or secretly, pledge their support even to the enemy solely for personal gain. There are those among our own tribes who indulge in pointless bickering and other forms of rebellion against leaders. Their interests are served at the cost of loyalty to the tribe or nation.

Now, if we are to become and remain the powerful nation that it lies within our potential to be, we must make radical changes in our ways of independence as tribes, as chieftains or as Huns who fail to make a contribution toward the unification that I, Attila, am bound by destiny to achieve.

Let it be known that I will no longer tolerate cunning of any nature among our Huns, chieftains or tribes that undermines the unification of our nation at any level or on any issue.

He who attempts such cunning and becomes known to me, or to any chieftain exercising authority over him, will hastily conform to our values or will be subjected to the most extreme reprimand.

While the coals of our campfires would long become dust before I could pronounce guidance and caution for all the evils a cunning Hun would bring upon us,

I shall provide you with counsel that is sufficient for your learning and understanding at this time.

- Beware of the treacherous Hun who pledges loyalty in public then spreads discontent in private. Make every effort to identify and remove these ignoble characters, be they chieftains or your best warriors.

- Be wise and anticipate the Brutus of your camp. Unfailing and ill-deserved loyalty to Brutus was fatally paid for by Caesar.

- Never expect your Huns to always be compatible. But expect their differences to be resolvable without the spread of discontent to other Huns.

- Never allow your Huns too many idle moments. These give rise to the beginnings of discontent.

- Never cast blame for failure upon the guiltless.

- Never allow your Huns to gain fame for the accomplished deeds of others.

- Never threaten the security or esteem of another Hun unless you are prepared to deal with the consequences.

- Be approachable; listen to both good and bad news from your Huns. Otherwise, you will provide reason for murmurings.

- Be principled, not inflexible.

- Be compatible to the policies of our nation and your tribe. Otherwise, you will seek devious ways to accomplish your own ambitions. Thus, you will ultimately lose, no matter how bold or tenacious your efforts.

- Reward Huns of character and integrity—they are rare.

- The spirit of unity must be a cardinal principle in the ways and attitudes of all Huns. Once divided, we are easily made subject to foreign nations.

In imparting this secret to success as leaders of Huns, I, Attila, charge you to be forthright in your demonstration of unity and to hold in contempt any who spread discontent among our tribes.

The unification of our tribes into a strong and formidable nation can only be realized through loyalty to our cause and to those who reign with responsibility over the destiny of our mighty horde.

# 6

# *The Tribute: "Paying and Receiving Deference"*

**A**ttila was well-schooled in the power of rumor. He knew that advantageous rumor in the hearts and minds of ten could result in thousands becoming his victims. Thus, through rumor, many obstacles to his "great conquest" could be removed.

He considered himself to be above the reproach of the masses; therefore, his reputation was important to him and him alone. He knew who he was, what he could achieve; his reputation was not as important to his feelings of self-worth as it was to influencing the outcome of battles and negotiations. Thus, Attila turned a nickname that in certain circles might have been considered unflattering into an advantage and, in doing so, gained riches for his treasury and tribute from untold thousands.

As the story goes, a Gallic monk, provoked either by

the horror of Attila's ambition or by a taste for mar-
tyrdom, created a new title for him. The monk hailed
Attila not as "King of Huns" but as "the Scourge of
God."

Attila, sensing the power this newly acquired title
would yield on the battlefield and in negotiations, was
quick to adopt it, for he knew the sobriquet would have
the influence of an army of 100,000.

Attila pressed the advantage of his reputation as "the
Scourge of God," counting on the fear inspired by rumor to guarantee the success of a well-planned tactic
to obtain needed moneys. In the year A.D. 446, Attila,
preparing to launch his march on the empire, needed
money to gain the supplies and materiel essential for
the expansion of his army. So he invaded Thessaly. His
goal was to ransom money from Theodosius II.

Selecting the most vicious and ferocious-looking
warriors from his army, Attila ordered them to wear
garb of rough fur and leather, to eat only raw meat
and to inflict the most horrible tortures on their prisoners. All of this planned fury was for the sake of per-
petuating a legend.

Resolved to fight the Huns that he mistakenly believed he had conquered five years earlier when the
horde halted within reach of the capital and were on
the verge of ravaging the empire, and with the audacity
and determination of a weakling annoyed at the dis-
ruption of his pleasure, Theodosius allowed the utter
destruction of more than seventy villages before he
sought to make a truce at Thermopylae.

Because of Theodosius' earlier resistance and now
his meek submission of the Eastern Roman Empire,
Attila raised the price of peace. Roman prisoners were

to be freed at a new cost of twelve pieces of gold instead of the usual eight.

Attila could have demanded much more. However, he knew the Romans would simply slap their subjects with new taxes to recoup the moneys. Attila had no wish to burden the peasants, merchants, artisans, plebeians or subjects of the empire, he simply sought to conquer its corrupt leaders.

## ATTILA ON: "PAYING AND RECEIVING DEFERENCE"

It is noble to accord the proper courtesy and recognition of stature to one in an office over you. And it is wise to pay deference to your peers and subordinates as well.

If a chieftain does not command the respect of his Huns and that of his foes, he is weak and held to be undeserving of his title.

Respect may be born of fear, real or perceived, as in my notoriety as "the Scourge of God." When deference is born of fear, however, it results in an unwillingness to serve and becomes manifested as passive resistance to authority and purpose. It further leads to subversion, to sabotage and to generally low morale among those you are attempting to lead.

Real deference results in unyielding loyalty—a tribe full of spirit and willing to follow their chieftain into the mouth of hell, if necessary, for the cause of the nation.

A chieftain's office is accepted by all as a position of

greater privileges because of increased responsibilities. Who of you would aspire to such an office if it brought no greater merit or privilege than that of an ordinary Hun?

Our system of deference prescribes recognized advantages as reward for effort, enterprise and accomplishment. The Hunnish people will acknowledge the privilege attending our various offices of leadership only so long as the demanded deference is reasonable and poses no harm to them. They are willing to grant such deference to those brave enough to lead the way. For they themselves see such respect as a cheap price to pay someone else to take on the responsibilities of leadership.

I must caution you, however, there are subtle aspects of paying and receiving deference that will make the deciding difference in one who leads by notoriety and one who leads with nobility. My words of counsel are:

■ Always accept the responsibility and privilege of your office seriously. Never should you exercise your authority to the disadvantage of your subordinates. Never should you exact more privilege from your office than your subordinates are willing to grant.

■ You are your reputation! If people speak evil of you, erroneously attribute misdeeds to you and will not serve a greater purpose, you must do away with those adversaries or you must behave in a manner that will encourage them to amend their judgments. It isn't easy being the Scourge of God, but it has its advantages in dealing with the enemy. Among my own people, however, I seek no such reputation. For if they perceived me as having such a wicked intent, I would not long serve as their king.

■ The king may use his fury and power to gain tribute from the enemy; however, a chieftain has no such privilege. Although, as king, I must rely on my chieftains to wisely use their power to influence the actions of their Huns, I, Attila, will hastily remove any chieftain who supposes similar influence over me.

■ Never should a chieftain fret over privilege. The responsibilities of office should always prevail. Deference comes to the chieftain who does not seek it for the sake of privilege alone.

■ The deference that attends any office of leadership is confirmed by custom, yet it is modified by circumstance. What stands as privilege in the court or palace seldom has utmost importance on the battlefield or in foreign territory. Be aware of where you are and whom you are with when exercising the privileges of your leadership position.

■ Any promotion will require an adjustment on your part as well as on the part of those who remember you in your former role. Have patience with yourself and others. Dignity of person and title is a noteworthy attribute in this situation.

■ Always pay proper courtesy to your subordinate leaders. Should you fail to accord them respect, so will their subordinates.

■ Paying deference to your adversaries is essential. Once you fail to recognize their abilities, influence and potential, they may gain advantage over you. Even as I was underestimated by Theodosius, it was I, Attila, who exacted tribute from his kingdom.

With this counsel, I share with you chieftains the duty of seeing to it that every position of leadership is paid deference appropriate to its incumbent responsibilities and that this deference is acceptable to those Huns whom we serve and respected by our adversaries, the Romans. Nevertheless, lest we become trapped in our own importance, do not underestimate the power of the empire to influence the course of the Hunnish nation.

# Battle Dress and Armament: "Chieftains Are as They Appear to Their Huns"

**A**ttila's presence was felt wherever he rode or rested. He was not only a Hun, he was the most distinguished Hun of all.

Scorning the pompous garb of noble Romans, Attila attired himself in the simple, crude skins of animals, which was the custom of his people. Even his crown, as king, was one of a simple leather helmet adorned by only a single feather. It was headgear similar to that of his warriors.

He rode upon the mighty and gallant black charger Villam ("Lightning"). So majestic an animal was Villam, it is said that grass never grew again on the path he trod. Villam was stronger and swifter than the mount of any other Hun. This was a necessity, for Attila had to ride first into battle, at the front of the horde. He was, after all, their leader. Villam served Attila bravely and displayed a certain magnificence that appealed to the Huns.

In battle, Attila was armed with the customary bow, lance and lariat of the Huns. His sword was another matter.

According to legend, during the dispute over who would succeed Bleda as king, a flaming sword appeared, firmly lodged in the ground in the midst of a meadow. Attila and others went to look upon this magical sword. As Attila held out his hand to grasp it, the sword "jumped" into his palm. The brilliance of the sword and its craftmanship far excelled that of any weapon made by a common man. Certainly it must be an omen: The Sword of God was sent to confirm Attila as King of Huns. Legend has it that he carried this mighty sword into all subsequent battles.

The Huns identified with Attila; his appearance was not markedly different from theirs. Yet, Villam and the Sword of God were sufficient to distinguish him as one destined to lead, to be followed and to be respected for his noble role, which was one of distinction and proper appreciation for the privileges of office.

# ATTILA ON:
## "CHIEFTAINS ARE AS THEY APPEAR TO THEIR HUNS"

Life in the Roman court and my understanding of the durable nature of Huns has served me well in learning how essential it is that a chieftain or king appear as is expected and acceptable to those he serves and those he chooses to impress.

Roman leaders adorn themselves in a manner that

is pompous, one that is unnatural to their constituency and repulsive to their allies. They, by their very appearance, ignite the spirit of their enemy to destroy such trappings of unwarranted superiority.

It is the custom of all followers to expect their leaders to be marked at times with armament that distinguishes them from the masses in the court or on the battlefield.

It is wise, however, that such distinction not be offensive to warriors and not provide the fuel to ignite the destructive spirit of the opposition in negotiations or on the field of battle.

Therefore, as we chat around this campfire, lighted for your learning and understanding, I will share my observations with you concerning the appearance of chieftains.

- A chieftain neither dresses nor arms himself at the expense of his Huns. His dress and weaponry may be of subtle distinction as is accepted by custom. Yet it must never be offensive in its cost or in its style, nor should its intent be to project ignoble superiority over those he leads, lest they scorn him for it.

- A chieftain should choose a well-made sword, not one glittering with jewels and gold but one honed to a sharp edge and made of the finest material in the land. A sword is the mark of a chieftain. His sword, like the chieftain himself, must prevail in battle. A chieftain should dress in fine skins and furs—not those draped by gold and silver adornments. Pompous appearance breeds hate and gives rise to contempt and laughter among the ranks.

- If it is necessary to appear as ferocious savages in order to project courage and victorious purpose, then do it well. Huns and chieftains should wear the most barbaric of all furs, robes and other apparel. Such appearance further serves to destroy the will of the enemy.

- If it is appropriate to dress as peaceful, pastoral peoples for the purpose of reign in your camp or in negotiations with strangers, lay aside your barbaric attire and clothe yourself in furs and robes fitting the occasion.

- When on the hunt, be prepared to hunt. Take your best bow and lance. Wear the clothing that will serve you well as you chase the wild beasts in the forest.

- On the occasion of celebration, it is customary for a chieftain to wear his finest furs and well-tanned skins. Again, an ignoble, superior attitude will only evoke disdain from the gathered and distract from the celebration.

- A chieftain who appears to be noble will be treated as such by both Hun and foe.

- One who appears as a jester of the courts will receive deference as the same.

These observations have served me well as your king. Insignificant as they may seem, dress and armament are important to a chieftain and will be counted in the measure of your success or failure.

# 8

# *Aetius: "Picking Your Enemies Wisely"*

**A**etius' father, a battlefield captain of high regard known as Master of the Horse and the Count of Africa, was murdered by his own soldiers during a revolt in Gaul. A German from Pannonia, his father wed a daughter of a wealthy royal Roman family. Thus, Aetius was both a son of a master warrior and of Roman nobility.

Sent to a foreign court as a child hostage, Aetius was received with honor by the Hunnish court of King Rugila in exchange for Attila.

In the court of Rugila, Aetius learned the ways of the Huns, their traditions, and gained insight into their collective personality. This learning would serve him and the empire well in future dealings with the Huns —particularly with Attila.

His relationship with King Rugila grew into a strong

bond. Later, he would convince Rugila to unite the armies of the Huns and ally them with John the Usurper, a Vandal by race, who had risen to become Master of Soldiers—a man Aetius thought capable of reuniting Rome and Constantinople.

Aetius cared little for the interests of a particular dynasty; an emperor meant much less than a cause.

On his return to Rome, Aetius wed the daughter of the patrician Carpilio. Always remaining on the best of terms with Rugila, Aetius became "Count of Domestics" and "Mayor of the Palace of Rome."

A man of unwavering principle, Aetius was physically strong, an expert in the art of war—a formidable warrior in every aspect. He mastered the intellect of both Hun and Roman and learned well the strengths and vulnerabilities of both nations.

Aetius knew the hardships of life and was subjected to great personal and professional challenges throughout the course of his life. On more than one occasion, he was the target of hired cutthroats and escaped seemingly by a miracle.

The corruption of the empire affected Aetius to the point that he contemplated, more than once, changing his allegiance to the Huns. It was, however, his strong sense of duty and his oath to serve that harnessed his anxieties. Thus, he always remained true to the empire.

It was Aetius who later commanded the Roman forces on the Catalaunian Plains. There he combined his mastery of the art of war with his knowledge of the battle order and tactics of the Huns to inflict the first and only defeat ever suffered by Attila's army.

In time, the corruption of the Roman leaders overcame Aetius. His advice was not sought when Attila began his final campaign against Italy. The price of neglecting Aetius' counsel was the defeat of the empire in many battles.

Although he remained loyal to the end, Aetius, in his old age, was reluctant to lead the Roman army against Attila, whom he supported in his thoughts as a worthy opponent and a man in pursuit of a great destiny.

In the end, Aetius was the victim of an assassination ordered by the emperor he had so loyally served, Valentinian. The ignominious death of Aetius marked the end of a great general and the only man in the empire whom Attila held in high regard.

# ATTILA ON:
# "PICKING YOUR ENEMIES WISELY"

Now, you chieftains and Huns, I, Attila, have need to counsel you on how to choose your enemies.

Most conflicts in our lives lie within the Hunnish nation, between our tribes, our chieftains or among the people. Seldom is our real enemy a Roman. Only infrequently will an enemy from outside have the stature and skill of an Aetius that will enable him to defeat us on the battlefield or in diplomacy, for we are Huns.

Being somewhat wise in the ways of Huns, yet naive in the things that cause conflict, most of you are totally unaware when you make enemies.

If you would set aside your tendencies to be unwilling to yield to another when appropriate, to let your feelings of inadequacy and insecurity prevail in situations warranting reason, to let your vanity become expedient over appreciating others' worthy displays of competence, and if you would hesitate before inappropriately influencing others, we would have more peace in our camps and have our energies in harmony when we face the Romans and the formidable Aetius, whom I have chosen as my enemy.

In dealing with other Huns and particularly with the Romans, we must be cunning insofar as we should make enemies only with purpose. As I reflect on my observations and experience, it has served me well to be aware of a few dangers in making enemies without intent.

These pitfalls are perils to your effectiveness as chieftains and warriors. Learn these, my secrets, well.

- Do not expect everyone to agree with you—even if you are king.

- Do not waste stamina trying to negotiate with implacable, uncooperative enemies—conquer them by more effective means.

- Do not consider all opponents to be enemies. You may have productive, friendly confrontations, with others inside and outside your tribe.

- Do not try to conform everyone's behavior unless doing so is critical to tribal discipline or purpose.

- Do not delegate an assignment and then attempt to manage it yourself—you will make an enemy of the overruled subordinate.

- Do not lose your temper without advantageous reason.

- Do not underestimate the power of an enemy, no

matter how great or small, to rise against you on another day.

- Do not let your chosen enemy have the advantage in any situation.

- Do not neglect the opportunity to deceive your enemy. Make him think of you as a friend. Let him think of you as weak. Let him act prematurely. And never tell him anything.

- Do not make enemies who are not worthy of your every effort to render them into a state of complete ineffectiveness.

- Do not fail to use an enemy's weakness to your advantage. On the other hand, when it becomes apparent that an enemy is too formidable, retreat and return another day when you can conquer him.

- Do not insult unless you mean it.

It should be sufficient for all Huns to recognize that when they exercise unbridled antagonism, create useless jealousy and hatred of their very being, their actions may serve to persuade even friends to become foes. A chieftain will not be followed long by Huns who despise him.

A Roman of formidable power, unwisely made an active enemy, can rise to victory in diplomacy and on the battlefield, for he becomes willing to win at any cost, and our nation will suffer agonizing defeat, even as I, Attila, did at the Battle of Châlons.

# Leading the Charge: "Responsibilities of a Chieftain"

The Hunnish horde adapted a new spirit of unity during the reign of Attila, for he had applied seemingly simple principles to unite the tribes into a strong nation.

Setting aside the granting of high honors for individual achievement in favor of bestowing more noble rewards upon those loyal to the new, national objective, Attila laid the groundwork for the success of the budding culture.

No longer would chieftains have the option to pledge their loyalty to other than the Hunnish nation. Should they choose to do so, Attila would remove them from their office.

No longer would the Huns be tribes of nomads rambling through the countryside in search of booty. They had a new direction! They would rule the world.

Now, under Attila, the barbarians so dreaded by the

empire and even nations of afar* had a strategy for their wanderings.

When possible, Attila exploited his influence through diplomatic relations, skills he absorbed as a boy in the Roman court. But if he failed to gain his objectives by peaceful means, Attila would unleash the fury of his horde, then attempt new negotiations to bring villages and nations under his control.

Attila, with his magnetic force, influence and, perhaps, charm, through which he united the Huns was so awe-inspiring to his warriors and chieftains that he was worshipped by them—even as a god by some.

His power became so prevalent a force during his reign that chieftains, not wishing to offend him and face his fury, would simply yield to him without the slightest resistance.

By way of fulfilling the obligation of his title, Attila exhibited patience—not haste—and never showed a lack of prudent judgment; his plan had been formulated over years. It was a calculated scheme of sequenced events that resulted in Attila's short-lived but complete leadership over a nation of barbarians whom, for a time, the world held in fear.

# ATTILA ON: "RESPONSIBILITIES OF A CHIEFTAIN"

It has been my observation over the years that nations, tribes and lesser bands rise and fall on the strength of

---

*Loosely interpreted from history and legend, it may be surmised that the Great Wall of China was built to bar Mongolian hordes—perhaps even Attila's—from the vast mainland.

their leaders and on the ability with which their leaders carry out their responsibilities of office—seeking first the good of the people.

The corruption of the empire is largely a result of the glamorous yet empty life its leaders seek to lead. They have lost their sense of national purpose and employ foreign armies to carry out the responsibilities incumbent to the Roman Legion.

They seek to gain office and stature by political maneuverings, casting aside personal standards of excellence in achievement and high expectations for unity. Their leadership is, therefore, based on weakened foundations and shallow loyalties.

While we are a young nation as a unity of tribes, we have strong traditions that tie us mystically together. We must use this delicate alliance as a basis for powerful, lasting bonds that better serve our collective destiny.

Our leaders—you chieftains and valued warriors, gathered here this night—must learn the responsibilities of office.

As many of you are unschooled in what I, Attila, consider to be the responsibilities of leadership, I now grant you my counsel on this subject.

■ Chieftains and leaders in every subordinate office are responsible for establishing the atmosphere in which they lead. This atmosphere may have periods of change even as the seasons change. Nonetheless, unlike our lack of influence over the weather, our leaders can and must influence and control the spirit of our tribes.

■ Leaders are bound by the traditions of office to establish and follow the order under which their Huns are judged, rewarded, punished and constrained. Without such order, known to all Huns, the people will live in chaos.

- By their own actions, not their words, do leaders establish the morale, integrity and sense of justice of their subordinate commanders. They cannot say one thing and do another.

- Leaders must establish a high spirit of mutual trust among subordinates and with their peers and superiors.

- Leaders must attach value to high standards of performance and have no tolerance for the uncommitted.

- Leaders must expect continual improvement in their subordinates based on new knowledge and experiences.

- Leaders must encourage creativity, freedom of action and innovation among their subordinates, so long as these efforts are consistent with the goals of the tribe or nation.

- Leaders must provide direction to their Huns, never letting them wander aimlessly.

- Chieftains realize greater recognition and booty than their Huns. I, Attila, expect, therefore, more from them than from their people.

- Chieftains and subordinate leaders must learn the responsibilities of their office. Without such knowledge, how can they fulfill their duties?

- Chieftains must teach their Huns well that which is expected of them. Otherwise, Huns will probably do something not expected of them.

- Chieftains must inspect their Huns frequently in order to see that what is accomplished meets with what is expected.

- Chieftains should never misuse power. Such action causes great friction and leads to rebellion in the tribe or nation.

- Chieftains make great personal sacrifice for the good of their Huns.

- Chieftains must not favor themselves over their Huns when supplies are short.

- Chieftains must encourage healthy competition among their people, but must contain it when such becomes a detriment to tribal or national goals.

- Chieftains must understand that the spirit of the law is greater than its letter.

- Chieftains must never shed the cloak of honor, morality and dignity.

- Chieftains must never form selfish relationships and, therefore, take advantage of their subordinates, peers or superiors.

- Chieftains must hold a profound conviction of duty above all other ambitions.

Now, I could continue with my counsel regarding the responsibilities of leadership. It would be, however, difficult to remember more than this at one time.

The things I have told you this night are the secrets to leadership success at any level of office. They may seem to you to be common knowledge. Alas, they may be, but they are not so common in practice.

You must leave this campfire counsel with one thought and one thought only. That is, success is the result of hard work that overcomes all forms of disappointment and moments of discouragement. Success is not achieved through complex strategies. It is achieved only through conscientiously carrying out the duties of your office and exercising the responsibilities of leadership —nothing else will prevail.

Now, go to your Huns and arise tomorrow with a new determination to follow your leaders, to support your peers and to lead your subordinates, otherwise we are destined to be slaves of the empire.

# 10

## The Omen of Aquileia: "The Essentials of Decisiveness"

**A**quileia was an imposing sight. Resting high on a hillside, surrounded by a water obstacle, its walls high and thick, its city gates reinforced, it was a bastion of Italy. Aquileia was familiar with invasions. Over the years, it had held against the Germans and various Asiatic tribes.

Inside, it was fortified by a well-trained garrison. Its food reserves and magazines were sufficient to withstand long sieges. Its people were resolved not to surrender their vast treasures, acquired by trade and an abundant agriculture, to any invaders—no matter how imposing.

The Aquileians were inexperienced with the Huns. The terror with which they regarded the horde was largely the result of the tales of the Huns' devastating attacks on other villages and lands. Attila's army was great in number. It consumed the countryside as though it were a swarm of locusts.

Coming off, as they were, two previous swift victories against other fortified cities, the Huns became impatient with their siege of Aquileia. Food for man and beast became scarce. The horde was restless—ready to march on to greater Italy. The conquest of Aquileia, however, was essential to Attila's plan to crush the empire.

Morale became low. The tribal chieftains challenged Attila's tactics. Dead horses were eaten and rations reduced—the Huns' situation became more desperate with each passing day.

This was not the horde of the past. Attila had altered many of their traditional habits. Now, they were a disciplined army, led by a king who had the patience to have taken some forty years to unite them.

Attila called his battle captains together in an evening council. He announced that the cost of the siege had become too great. They would bypass Aquileia the next morning. At daybreak, the Huns would begin preparing for their march.

On the following day, taking a final look at the city he hoped to defeat at another time, Attila observed a stork flying out of Aquileia, driving a young brood before her. It was destiny—an omen that would turn the course of events.

Announcing that animals could sense things before men, Attila ordered his army to fulfill the presage of this omen from powers beyond man's comprehension. Now, instead of bypassing Aquileia, they would attack.

Equipped with catapults and tall ladders, the newly disciplined Hunnish horde executed a masterful attack. The city, despite its experience with and repellence of invasions in the past, fell. It was a swift victory. Aquileia was left in flames, its vast treasures added to the booty already overflowing Attila's chariots.

Destiny had been fulfilled through patience and the ability to sense the precise moment to act.

# ATTILA ON: "THE ESSENTIALS OF DECISIVENESS"

Our seasoned chieftains have become wise through experience as to when it is right to act and when it remains best to contemplate further. On the other hand, our young, ambitious Huns, anxious to demonstrate their deftness, will often precipitate actions that result in loss for them, their tribe and perhaps the nation.

Such rashness is unacceptable in those appointed to lead. All chieftains must learn that victory comes to one who knows not only what to do but when to do it.

Young Huns are taught skill in weaponry—mastering the bow, the lance, the lariat—and in horsemanship. They learn the advantage of swift action on the battlefield. They learn to be forthright in demonstrating these abilities.

As their mentors, we teach them to take the initiative, to have the moral courage and force that make the difference between followers and leaders. We must, however, demonstrate for them the main points possessed by the leader who travels the determining mile between sporadic and spurious accomplishment and resolute performance in all things. One of these points is decisiveness.

Now, I give you chieftains counsel for acquiring skill in decisiveness.

- Noble resolve to do the right thing is characteristic of prudent decision making. Responsible decisions are difficult to improve upon.

- Wise is the chieftain who never makes a decision when he doesn't understand the issue. In decision making, valor is guided by prudence.

- A chieftain should allow his subordinates the privilege of making decisions appropriate to their level of responsibility. Weak is the chieftain who reserves every decision for himself out of fear that he might lose control.

- The circumstances of a given moment are not to be used as an excuse for being unprepared to make decisions incumbent to a chieftain. Indecisiveness is bred by failure to accept the responsibility of office—be it great or small.

- A chieftain who fails to accept full decision-making responsibility—or who blames others for his own bad decisions—is weak and lacking in an essential, inherent quality of leadership.

- Rarely are there perfect decisions. The best decisions are usually the more prudent of the logical alternatives. When you must be overly persuasive in gaining support for your decision, it's usually a sign of a bad one.

- When the consequences of your decision are too grim to bear, look for another option. Compassion is the byword when making difficult decisions that, unavoidably, have temporary or long-lasting adverse consequences for even a few Huns.

- Next to the importance of knowing when to make a decision stands the insight to know when to forgo making one. Impatient chieftains often precipitate premature action.

- Perhaps the most critical element of decision making is timing. Prompt determination after appropriate deliberation is a worthy principle of decisiveness.

- In selecting an alternative, wise chieftains look for the choice in which the benefits outweigh the risks and costs of the decision. Noble chieftains make decisions in favor of the common good.

- Chieftains are to be cautioned against rushing to conclusions when there is time and opportunity to improve upon the basic decision.

- Wise chieftains often extract from obscure places the critical elements for making the right decision. The key is learning to find the obscure places and to recognize the critical elements.

- Skepticism has value in that it delays premature decision making. When a chieftain can't make up his mind, it's worthwhile to restate the problem.

- Chieftains should delegate only those decisions they want their subordinates to make. Conversely, chieftains who inappropriately make decisions for their subordinate leaders diminish the potential that exists for the young chieftains to learn and grow by exercising their judgments and being held accountable for the consequences of their decisions.

■ Initiative in decision making is not sufficiently demonstrated by a chieftain when it occurs only in relation to easy assignments. It must be exhibited when facing difficult and high-risk tasks as well. A sure sign of a weak chieftain is hesitation to act out of fear he might fail.

■ Doubt and delay are frequently symptomatic of chieftains promoted beyond their capacities. On the other hand, we often find ourselves in unfortunate situations in which too many chieftains make too many decisions with too little wisdom.

■ Chieftains must avoid decisions that favor themselves at the expense of the Huns. Every decision is an opportunity to improve the conditions of the Huns, the tribe and the nation.

■ Chieftains grow to understand that the wisdom of a particular decision can change with time. Make every effort, therefore, to improve future decisions by learning from those you've already made.

■ It takes less courage to criticize the decisions of others than to stand by your own.

■ Paradoxical as it may seem, sometimes the best decisions are made void of the emotions evoked by the facts bearing on the problem.

■ It is good to remember that chieftains are, in large, rewarded for the decisions they make. Huns, conversely, are, in large, rewarded for how well they support and carry out decisions.

- Self-confidence is critical to decisiveness, for without it, a chieftain loses his following in challenging situations.

- In the end, vision, drive, energy, singleness of purpose, wise use of resources and a commitment to a destiny worthy of his efforts become a character of a chieftain who excels.

You chieftains must make the extra effort and demonstrate rigor in developing a sense of decisiveness. Knowing by instinct or by fact when the time is right for action will yield a high measure of success. Decisiveness in leadership action carries a heavy burden. Often it means victory or defeat. We cannot hesitate to act, but neither can we prematurely precipitate decisions that will work to our disadvantage.

# 11

# Horse Holders: "The Art of Delegation"

**E**ven as the rider who dismounts and expects to return to his fiery steed requires a horse holder, it was necessary that Attila have assistance from his chieftains in order to attend to all of the responsibilities that demanded his attention.

In the early stages of his efforts to unify the various tribes, Attila sought to gain loyalty from easily allied chieftains. Thus, he would have the formidable power of numbers when he challenged more-powerful chieftains.

As king, he would not be capable of overseeing every action of his nation, its tribes and its chieftains. He would require the unfeigned loyalty of trusted chieftains to whom he could delegate responsibility.

The Hunnish nation had long been wandering, individual tribes that sold their services to any cause for a price, or for short-term gains of booty and perhaps even ephemeral moments of peace.

The chieftains and their tribes had lost some deference for Attila as a member of the Hunnish royal family for he had not been long in their camps, as his childhood had been spent in the court of the Romans as a hostage.

Waiting patiently, as a spider waits for its prey, Attila used his time to develop sufficient loyalties and a following that would yield him chieftains to whom he could delegate national unification responsibilities. This he could do with a minimum of risk that they would cast their lots once again with other chieftains or with foreign leaders.

Risk in delegation was high; however, without accepting such a risk Attila would, alas, have been destined to rule over only the tribe of his royal family, and his greater ambition to unify the tribes into a powerful nation would have been lost.

# ATTILA ON:
## "THE ART OF DELEGATION"

Our nation cannot prevail as the dominant world power if its leadership is contained to one man. Even I, Attila, cannot accomplish for you what you are not willing to accomplish for yourselves. You must be willing to accept the responsibilities that I choose to delegate to you. At the same time, your charters are too great for you to accomplish alone. You must trust to your subordinate leaders those responsibilities that fit their office.

Ours is too great and too complex a nation for even such as I, Attila, to direct and lead every action. I must entrust you with certain important duties as chieftains of your various tribes. If I cannot, we are destined to wander as small bands of nomads.

This gathering is for the purpose of my imparting to you my counsel regarding the leadership principle of delegation, which is central to your success as chieftains.

Judgment, experience and the incumbent duties of office dictate the order of delegation. I cannot supply counsel that applies to each act of delegation. Nonetheless, I can provide counsel useful to you in the act and art of delegation.

Learn these precepts well, or your burden will be too great to accomplish those responsibilities in your charge.

- Chieftains should never delegate responsibilities necessitating their direct attention.

- Those actions that don't require a chieftain's direct handling are appropriately delegated to the one most able to fulfill the assignment.

- Wise chieftains grant both authority and responsibility to those they have delegated assignments.

- Wise chieftains always hold their subordinates accountable for delegated assignments.

- Worthy chieftains accept full responsibility for all assignments—even those they have delegated to their subordinates.

- Once a chieftain has delegated responsibilities, he should never interfere, lest his subordinates come to believe that the duties are not truly theirs. Such superficial delegation yields fury in the hearts of subordinates.

- When asked to, a chieftain should assist a subordinate with his delegated tasks—otherwise the subordinate may fail because he is not yet of the mettle necessary to fulfill the assignment.

■ Realize that a chieftain cannot accomplish every responsibility of his office by himself. Should he prove otherwise, a leader should understand that he is, in fact, chieftain over little or nothing at all.

■ A competent chieftain will delegate important assignments to even inexperienced subordinates in order that he might accomplish his mission, develop his subordinates' skills and demonstrate loyalty for and trust in his subordinates.

■ A chieftain should surround himself with subordinates to whom he feels comfortable delegating assignments. Otherwise, he must perform the incumbencies of both his and their offices.

■ A chieftain should never punish a subordinate who has failed if he did his best to carry out a delegated responsibility.

■ Chieftains should encourage their subordinates to use creativity to fulfill delegated responsibilities.

■ Subordinates will never develop their skills if their chieftain precisely directs them how to accomplish their delegated assignments.

■ A wise chieftain expands his influence and ability to serve the nation only through the art of delegation.

More counsel on this subject escapes me at this time. Perhaps it is best, for I wish not to underwhelm you with weakening thoughts.

# 12

# Booty: "Rewarding Your Huns"

Long hostages of a nomadic life, dependent for survival upon whatever booty they had stored in their chariots, the Huns were inspired by the glory and spoils that stemmed from the exploitation of their deeds as intrepid warriors.

Booty, the spoils of victory, was for many tribes the mainstay of their existence; they themselves were subject to being swept from conquered lands by nations who also relished the luxuries gained by vanquishing others.

Often, their appetites for glory and pillage gained from victorious battle caused them to forget their gods and heroes and diminished their perspective of national goals. Looting was, for the Huns, simply a part of postbattle etiquette.

More than the prepayment of servitude, the Huns

were attracted by the novel uncertainties of pillage. War was their method of survival. Their nomadic life required periodic replenishment gained for them through pillage when the storehouses that were their chariots grew bare.

Attila understood these customs. He knew the Huns were driven by intrinsic desires so strong that, simply to enjoy the spoils of war, the tribes would often become mercenaries for foreign nations and march in campaigns against even other Hunnish tribes.

His role was to harness this desire for short-term gain—to use discipline in the distribution of booty as reward for energies spent for the good of the Hunnish nation—as he set out to realize his people's formidable potential.

## ATTILA ON:
## "REWARDING YOUR HUNS"

Booty has become a powerful force that ignites the spirits of our warriors, driving them to commit their talents to any nation that bribes them into service.

You, as leaders of your tribes, and I, Attila, as King of Huns, must turn this lust for booty into a more disciplined distribution of rewards to Huns who willingly give their services to our nation either in or out of battle.

Booty, as such, is most often a short-lived benefit to which our Huns have become accustomed as their wages of war. We must continue to grant unto our warriors their rights of pillage and at the same time provide rewards for acts off the battlefield that we endorse.

Controlling the undisciplined desire for booty among our horde is necessary for our civilization to triumph over barbaric customs. For this purpose I, Attila, issue guidance on rewarding your Huns.

- Never reward a Hun for doing less than is expected of him. Otherwise, he will doubt your sincerity in rewarding appropriate acts and, even worse, expect reward for performing deeds for which you hold no approval.

- Never reward a Hun for every act completed correctly. Otherwise, he will not act in the absence of your presence or without the certainty of recognition.

- Grant small rewards for light tasks. Reserve heaps of booty for dangerous, gallant, substantial effort and worthy accomplishment.

- Praise those who are simply good Huns. Their need for gratification tends to parallel their level of ambition. Security is utmost for those who risk not. Give them, therefore, assurance—not great booty—lest they learn large value is given to those who just get by.

- Sincere concern for and purposeful mingling with your Huns will raise their spirits and encourage greater valor.

- Teach your Huns that the booty of battle is nothing more than wages for their service. Heaps of booty, promotion through the ranks and recognition as being a mighty warrior are reserved for those who go beyond the normal call of duty.

■ Grant your Huns the benefit of your interest in the welfare of their families and the condition of their stores; share your riches with those who are loyal and stand in need. They will be certain to willingly follow you into the mouth of hell, should the occasion arise.

■ Care more for the rewarding of your Huns than for rewarding yourself. Your own rewards will then far exceed even your greatest hopes and dreams.

■ Never give a Hun a reward that holds no value for yourself.

■ Never underestimate the ability of the empire or other foes to gain the support and loyalty of Huns you fail to heed and rightfully reward.

■ Be generous with small tokens of appreciation—they will multiply in returned loyalty and service.

Now, I cannot provide counsel as to the appropriateness of every reward for every situation. You, as chieftains, must develop your own judgments, based upon these principles, into a system of disciplined rewards that will weld the loyalty of your Huns.

# 13

## Attila and the Pope: "The Art of Negotiation"

The combination of sparse rations, contaminated water supplies, intense heat, illness and general listlessness had wrought its toll upon the spirit of the Hunnish horde in the year A.D. 452. The Italian campaign, though unexpectedly successful for Attila's army, was taxing the Huns' endurance.

In the Roman court, Valentinian ignored the counsel of Aetius, who had fallen from favor. After questioning his generals and senators, Valentinian judged the Roman army to be incapable of a victorious engagement with Attila's newly reorganized army. Suing for peace seemed the only hope for the survival of Rome.

But who could Valentinian send to negotiate with the mighty Attila? For whom did Attila hold enough respect that the petition for peace would even be considered?

The Christian world held vast reverence for Pope Leo I. He was a man of God, of eloquence and culture, and had even been consulted by the Emperor Valentinian in times of difficulty.

Attila's army was marshaled at Mantua. Surely Rome would soon be in flames, her storehouses emptied and her treasury pillaged by the horde. It was a time for urgent action.

Valentinian called upon the aging pope to gather a cortege, then to proceed to Attila's camp and sue for peace and the sparing of Rome—the last stronghold of the empire.

The tactic dumbfounded Aetius. He knew Attila's army would fall as it had at Châlons if the empire would but stall. Aetius, however, was not consulted, and Valentinian's plan was put into action.

On the other side of the impending battle, Attila was hesitant. He feared another defeat by the Romans. Yet his fury was fired by the humiliations he had suffered in his youth in Rome. His oath, taken silently as a child, was to someday destroy the palace, triumphal arches and churches in Rome, a city for which he held contempt.

A scout returned to Attila's camp and told of the advance of the Roman army. In quick order, the now-disciplined horde was readied. The march to a final encounter with the legions of Rome began.

Soon after the Huns moved out, the scout returned again. Bewildered, he reported to Attila that it was not the empire's legions but a procession of priests and monks that approached. It was being led by an old man with a white beard, dressed in white, upon a white steed.

Calling a halt to the horde's advance, Attila, atop the gallant black charger Villam, rode forward with a few warriors to inquire as to the nature of this unexpected delegation.

Halting his warriors on the banks of a river, Attila challenged the stranger as to his name. "Leo" was the reply.

It was Attila who rode through the stream to approach this unusual emissary of the Roman court.

There, on the far bank, Attila and the pope held a counsel whose content has never been revealed.

For whatever reasons history or legend may give, it was the destiny of Rome to be spared. For, after a time, Attila returned to his mighty horde and turned its march first northward and then back to their homeland in the valley of the Danube.

# ATTILA ON:
## "THE ART OF NEGOTIATION"

The techniques of negotiation are not easily taught. It is for both Hun and chieftain to learn skills useful in negotiating. These are mastered only through understanding gained by experience.

My negotiations at a time when victory seemed so apparent to my chieftains and warriors, anxious to pillage Rome, were a mystery to them. But it was to our advantage to grant respite.

Your naïveté about the ways of negotiation prevents you from understanding my actions with the pope and the subsequent withdrawal of our army from Italy. For this purpose I, Attila, gather you in this council to enlighten you as to how to conduct yourself at those times when you will be required to negotiate for the good of your Huns and tribes and perhaps our nation.

Now I give to all assembled my counsel, in the hopes that it will serve to add to your wisdom and your expertise in the leader's vital art of negotiation.

- Always maintain the diplomatic initiative in all negotiations. Be on the offense always—never lose contact with your enemy. This will place him in a lesser position, and you will have the upper hand.

- Always negotiate at the lowest level possible. This will serve to resolve small things before they grow out of proportion and make negotiating impossible.

- Never trust negotiation to luck. Enter every session armed with knowledge of the enemy's strengths and weaknesses; knowing his secrets makes you strong and allows you to better deceive him as to your ultimate goals.

- Keep negotiations secret! They must be conducted in private—even as I did with Pope Leo. Only the policies should become public knowledge. How they were negotiated should remain confidential, saving loss of face.

- Time is your ally when you're negotiating. It calms temperaments and gives rise to less-spirited perspectives. Never rush into negotiations.

- Never arbitrate. Arbitration allows a third party to determine your destiny. It is a resort of the weak.

- Never make negotiations difficult on immediate, lesser

points, at the cost of a greater outcome. Acquiescence on lesser issues softens the spirit of your adversary.

- In negotiation you must take well-studied risks. Try to foresee all possible outcomes to determine those that will yield favorable results.

- Be aware of the temperament in your foe's camp. Take advantage of troubles and turmoils that arise during negotiations.

- Never overestimate your own adroitness. You may simply be negotiating with a weak opponent. Though fortuitous, this will not always be the situation.

- Never intimidate.

- Honor all commitments you make during negotiations lest your enemy fail to trust your word in the future.

- Remember, agreement in principle does not dictate agreement in practice. It does, however, serve to save face at the moment.

- Be bold in facing the inevitable. Acquiesce when resistance would be pointless or when your victory can be gained only at too high a cost. Of this you may not approve, but it is your duty to do so for the good of all Huns.

- Be keenly aware of time. Present appealing alternatives that are appropriate to your opponent's situation at the moment of your negotiations. Otherwise, he will dismiss your propositions.

Now, you mighty chieftains must come to an understanding of a final simple fact. It is never wise to gain by battle what may be gained through bloodless negotiations. Reserve the potential loss of your warriors for great causes not attainable without waging battle.

With these thoughts, I end this council on the art of negotiation. Remember this time together in order that you may always exact negotiations for the betterment of our nation as we fulfill our destiny of conquering all before us.

# 14

## Surviving Defeat: "There Is Another Day"

**T**hough not unfamiliar with toil, struggle, deception and other challenges that regularly attend leaders, Attila was unprepared for and unaccustomed to defeat on the battlefield.

It was Aetius, his lifelong foe, who had so skillfully led the Roman Legion at the Battle of Châlons, who tore Attila's mighty horde apart and caused them to retreat.

Attila's will snapped! His confidence in his destiny deserted him! He turned his sights within, ignoring for a time the confusion, shouting and wailing that accompanied the shaken horde as they strayed to safer ground.

Wandering about his camp in contemplation of the errors of the day, Attila was demoralized in this, the darkest moment of his reign. Was he to become the victim of a lost cause? Was he no longer master of the world?

Experiencing all of the inner turmoil concomitant with great disappointments, Attila was suffering as all responsible leaders do on such occasions.

Yet, drawing upon his inner strengths of dogged tenacity, determination and extraordinary will, Attila marshaled his emotional stamina and regained control of himself.

He would not be distracted from his ambitions! He would reorganize his armies! Introduce new customs to his nation! The Huns would rise again! There would be another day!

## ATTILA ON: "THERE IS ANOTHER DAY"

I, Attila, King of Huns, have called this assembly of chieftains and mighty warriors together for the purpose of encouragement. Further, my aim is to kindle the fires of your emotional stamina so that you may not become hopeless in the face of disappointment.

It has been a sad experience for me to suffer so great a defeat as handed me by Aetius. Although I am familiar with the loneliness of command, with betrayal by those I have trusted and with moments of trouble, I was simply not prepared to suffer the anguish of so paramount a defeat—and my consequent bewilderment—as met me on the Catalaunian Plains.

It is, therefore, incumbent to my office that I prepare you chieftains and future chieftains to deal with disappointment and discouragement.

Your understanding of my internal suffering and then renewed determination after the Battle of Châlons is perhaps not well served by a detailed account at this time.

Rather, I will provide you with specific counsel that may become useful in dealing with your own future challenges, for only I can deal with my own defeat.

Therefore, let these guiding principles for dealing with defeat be known among you.

- No chieftain will ever win every encounter. It matters not whether it be in tribal leadership or on the battlefield, nor how great or insignificant is the issue at hand—sometimes you will lose, regardless of how prepared you are to win.

- Should you become aware that defeat on the battlefield or in negotiations is impending, don't deny it. Face it and take immediate action to minimize the opponent's gain and get back to your cause.

- Retreat is noble when continuance with the battle or the issue at hand would result in further losses or total annihilation of your resources. In order to return on another day, you must salvage all the warriors and materiels possible.

- Momentary loss of self-worth, -confidence and -determination are normal emotions that accompany personal loss. Learn that you must pass through this misery to rid your Hunnish spirit of its depression. Lament, if necessary, but do not dwell too long on your bad moments lest they rise to rule your emotions forever.

■ A wise chieftain avoids exposing his Huns to possible defeat if they are not yet prepared to deal effectively with disappointment.

■ It is wise to consider all potentialities of battle and negotiations before entering into them. Rehearse them in your mind. Think of the consequences that may result from your actions. This will allow you to be better prepared for the worst outcome.

■ Learn from defeat! If you fail to sharpen your leadership prowess after confronting unconquered obstacles, your experiences were for naught, and you, as well as your subordinates, will become nothing more than a helpless victim.

■ Always remember that worthy causes meet with the most resistance—even internal withholding of support and loyalty. If victory is easily gained, you must reconsider the worthiness of your ambitions.

■ It is a simple truth that the greater your accomplishments—your victories—the greater opposition, torment and discouragement your enemies will throw in your path. Expect it! Don't become a victim of it.

■ Know that your most worthy efforts will be scorned by your peers, for it is they who suffer most when you excel. If your actions and ambitions threaten them not, you're simply striving toward the insignificant.

■ Reserve a portion of your emotional stamina for those times when to overcome obstacles requires even your last resources. Never expend all your energies in the charge when retreat and regrouping has even the slightest potential of happening.

Alas, the campfire has dwindled on this gathering. Be it to your advantage that you learn from my agonies. Let these insights to my secrets be the fuel to ignite the fires of your determination to retreat and regroup your ambitions for success on another day. For as long as a Hun breathes, all is not lost.

# 15

## The Bones of Caravans Past: "Lessons Learned"

**B**y nightfall, the Catalaunian Plains were heaped with some 162,000 to 300,000 slain Huns, the aftermath of the Battle of Châlons, in which Attila's lifelong nemesis, Aetius, had dealt his army its only defeat.

Aetius had employed delay tactics at the start of the battle. He knew deceptiveness as to the moment and place where the main encounter would begin would irritate Attila and would weaken his army's morale and determination.

Frustrated by the delay in battle, the Huns finally charged in mid-afternoon. The earth shook as thousands upon thousands of Hunnish chargers pounded the ground, tearing headlong into battle.

The shields of the Roman army turned aside the

avalanche of arrows that Aetius knew would precede the axes and javelins of the horde.

The fury continued as the Huns, now dismounted, began hand-to-hand combat with the well-trained and -disciplined infantry under Aetius' command.

The Romans' bronze helmets and metallic body armor rendered the stone-headed axes of the horde useless. Their long lances and lariats served only to encumber the horde as the fighting turned savage.

Aetius had used his knowledge of Attila's tactics to the victorious advantage of the Latin and Frankish soldiers who composed his army.

The dazzling brilliance of his horde's accomplishments on battlefields past had not served Attila in his quest to annihilate the powerful enemy army and its leader, Aetius. Attila, unlike Aetius, had prepared neither himself nor his horde for the struggle so valiantly fought and lost on the Catalaunian Plains.

## ATTILA ON: "LESSONS LEARNED"

The dreaded enemy led by Aetius used tactics unfamiliar to our noble warriors on the Catalaunian Plains. Many of our brave Huns were lost in a battle for which I simply had not prepared them to fight.

We have held too long to a strategy marked by swift movement, dealing death from horseback with long lances and dragging the enemy to his end by our lariats. Our battle dress and armament has been designed to serve us only under such conditions. They are not suited for infantry warfare against soldiers equipped with shields, helmets and suits of armor. The swords of the enemy have proven superior to our stone axes.

Alas, ours was a plan more aligned with past victories. Our discipline and patience wore thin under the provocation of Aetius' stalling tactics. Our fury was prematurely unleashed, which led to our suffering defeat. We are unaccustomed to losing. We are winners. We must examine the now sun-bleached bones of our lost warriors. We must regroup and emerge with renewed vigor and purpose and return to deal defeat to our enemy.

As we howl for our lost ones and ponder our sufferings, we must likewise learn the mighty lessons in them if we are to rise up with the strength of spirited warriors who want not to be at the mercy of the Romans!

Now, I, Attila, must relay to you the learning I accumulated in my study of the bones of caravans past.

- Our army must become more commandable in battle. We must create a new battle plan with a better arrangement of our chieftains and Huns. We must use tactics that control our maneuvers.

- We must refrain from charging prematurely and furiously into unfamiliar situations.

- We must not be unprepared for new tactics employed by the enemy. We must watch him closely, using our intelligence, to detect and assess his likely methods.

- When we are outfitted in battle dress and armament of inferior utility, we must never engage an enemy. Future battles with the Romans demand us to cover our leather helmets with metal, to reinforce our bodies with metal breastplates and to carry shields to turn away the blows of swords. We must use newly forged swords and cast aside our obsolete stone axes.

- Our adroitness as cavalrymen must be supplemented by newly acquired infantry skills. Training in these tactics will balance our abilities to wage war.

- We must add catapults to our arsenal. We cannot expect the high walls of Roman bastions to crumble at the simple beating of our chargers' hoofs.

- We cannot presume to rule over the Romans and conquer the world as wandering tribes of nomads. We must build cities. These cities must be fortified centers for our planning. From them we will send out well-disciplined and -trained armies—well supplied and armed with the new weapons of a superior arsenal.

- We cannot expect to change our long-held traditions, to reorganize our army and to create great cities without internal opposition. Among you chieftains and Huns will be those whose spirits cling to our past ways. We will show patience with you unenlightened ones. Yet, if you choose not our new course and cause dissension, you will be stricken from our ranks.

- Our vision of the future must build on the strength of the past. Yet, we must anticipate new challenges and opportunities. Suffering another Battle of Châlons is unacceptable to me as your king and to our people, who depend on us, their leaders and warriors, to serve their interests and ambitions.

■ We must never fail to analyze the past. No bleached bone of a battle-lost Hun must go unnoticed as we prepare for the future by laying aside the ill-conceived and undisciplined strategies of our past. We must form new policies and practices into a Hunnish unity of well-defined purpose. We must plan to once again and forever excel against all enemies and overcome obstacles that stand in the way of our conquering the world.

Now, in ending my counsel on lessons learned from the study of bones of caravans past, I leave you with a parting bit of wisdom. No radical change is easy. Radical change is only necessary when we fail to learn from our past in anticipating the future. The greatest adversary to abandoning the ineffectiveness of our past is a reluctance among yourselves to demonstrate the spirited support of your king, who seeks for you a new trail toward achieving things good for all Huns.

# 16

## Ashes to Ashes: "Departing with Nobility"

**H**is death came unexpectedly. It happened at a time when he was about to lead his reorganized and formidable army into a new quest to conquer the empire.

Attila was dead! His warriors and chieftains were stunned! Women wept! Children feared! Their noble king was gone forever! The Hunnish nation had prematurely lost its central figure of unity, pride and leadership.

Although still in shock, the high priests prepared for the burial ceremony. As Attila lay on a high bier in the main square of Etzelburg, a black horse was offered in sacrifice as the sightless high priest Kama asked the departed Hunnish spirits how their king should be buried. The answer directed that Attila be buried in a triple coffin: the first of gold like the sun; the second of silver, as the tail of a comet; the third of iron, for Attila was of iron. To prevent any threat of disturbance of the beloved king in his final rest, Kama was told by the spirits to bury Attila at the bottom of the Tisza River. A dam was constructed to divert a small channel of the river, and a grave was prepared in the riverbed.

As thousands sang mournful songs and shouted mingled cries, the funeral wagon was led to the grave site by twelve black horses, preceded by a riderless Villam saddled and draped with black cloth. The royal family, nobles, chief warriors and bareheaded Hun grandees followed the coffin on foot.

Joined by people from allied nations, some having traveled as long as three days, the sea of mourners carried thousands of torches as the sun descended in the western sky. Then, with a roll of drums and final blasts of tribute from his army's bugles, Attila was laid to rest. The dam was broken, and the waters rushed to protect the site from all future evil.

A legend was gone. In the future, his name would be held in both high esteem and contempt, but he would long be remembered for his deeds as Attila, King of Huns.

# ATTILA ON:
## "DEPARTING WITH NOBILITY"

Being assigned to any position of leadership over our Huns or tribes is gratifying. Worthy leaders fill the void between what Huns can do without a leader and what they can accomplish with one. Each chieftain is unique, marked by his mannerisms and his personal commitment to fulfill the obligations assumed in accepting his office.

It is soon after a new chieftain is appointed that he will either grow or diminish in the eyes of his subordinates, peers and superiors. If he is prudent in the application of his authority, demonstrates a spirit of commitment and sees to it that all obligations are met, the chieftain will enlarge his stature. Then, he will have gained personal loyalty, trust, confidence and respect from all Huns under his command, from his peers and superiors. Some truly outstanding chieftains may even stir up jealousy in those leaders who are less capable in their positions.

Nonetheless, a strong bond will develop between a true chieftain and his Huns. They will begin to emulate him, perhaps speak of him in their casual conversation. They may make him the subject of tales reflecting his courage, persona and accomplishments. In the end, they will ride into the mouth of hell for him, for he becomes more than an ordinary chieftain—he becomes their chieftain, one they are proud to serve.

As time passes, it is the tendency for both chieftain and Huns to cloud their objectiveness of perception and fail to remember that the incumbent in any position of leadership is subject to ephemeral assignments. Either a new assignment, old age or death will eventually remove even the most tenured and greatest chieftain from his office.

Thus, it is a tender moment in the lives of all who have developed strong bonds of loyalty and dedication when the former chieftain passes on and a new one is appointed in his place. This transition of leadership, influence and power must be made with the adroitness of diplomacy and protocol to serve the good of the Huns, tribe and nation. For this purpose, I provide this counsel to both chieftains and Huns regarding departure with nobility.

- It is the wise chieftain who prepares himself for the eventual moment when his time has passed and a new chieftain is about to take charge. This preparation should be made over time, to avoid precipitating insecurity or loss of commitment or dissipating confidence.

- It is noble for the departing chieftain to express gratitude to all who have served him well, especially recognizing ways in which they have made him stronger and more resilient.

- It is noble for Huns to honor their departing chieftain, giving recognition and appreciation for his service to them.

- It is noble for the departing chieftain to voice his confidence that the new chieftain will serve his Huns well, perhaps even improving their conditions. This expression, even if offered in a token fashion, reduces moments of insecurity and worry for the Huns who remain.

- It is noble for the departing chieftain to leave his command forever, never attempting to return by influencing the Huns once in his command. In doing so, he would subvert the leadership authority and responsibility of the new chieftain. Such action by the old chieftain would be destructive, even if invited by seemingly innocent appeal from Huns who once trusted his counsel. Every appeal of this nature should be denied, and the former chieftain should reaffirm his commitment to the new one by directing the Huns to seek counsel from their rightful leader.

- Regardless of the conditions under which a former chieftain departs his camp—no matter how distasteful or dishonorable—the new leader should neither encourage nor tolerate disrespectful talk of him. Speaking ill will not change past events or serve to further the Huns' understanding. It will most certainly tarnish the stature of the new leader.

- If departure should come prematurely, without warning or preparation to receive a new chieftain, tremendous confusion will reign in the camp. This is the most difficult situation for all. Those who rank highest, the senior Huns and chieftains, must quickly form a council and choose a new leader. For, in dire circumstances, our Huns look to their chieftain for strength, courage and direction.

Even as I, Attila, King of Huns, must someday be succeeded in my reign, my reflections and memories will be sweet only if I feel I have prepared the nation for this inevitable moment. And, if I have prepared you well, you will continue to be a nation of united tribes who seek to improve life for the Huns. For loyalty should not be solely placed in a man—no matter his personal magnetism. Loyalty of the Huns should have balance in the commitment of all to serve as a unified nation of Huns without hesitation, no matter who reigns over you.*

*It is perhaps important for the reader to understand that Attila had no successor of his capability. No chieftain or prince emerged after his death who possessed the richness of his views or the depth of his commitment. The Huns became divided again, most tribes resumed their nomadic life, battles were lost and the once strong nation was absorbed into greater Europe. The vanity of the princes and chieftains who jealously sought to succeed him resulted in the downfall of the nation. They had simply failed to learn from Attila—seeking first their own interests rather than those of the nation.

# Attilaisms:
# Selected Thoughts
# of Attila

## ADVICE AND COUNSEL

- Written reports have purpose only if read by the king.

- A king with chieftains who always agree with him reaps the counsel of mediocrity.

- A wise chieftain never kills the Hun bearing bad news. Rather, the wise chieftain kills the Hun who fails to deliver bad news.

- A chieftain who asks the wrong questions always hears the wrong answers.

- A wise chieftain never asks a question for which he doesn't want to hear the answer.

# CHARACTER

- The greatness of a Hun is measured by the sacrifices he is willing to make for the good of the nation.

- A chieftain should always rise above pettiness and cause his Huns to do the same.

- A chieftain cannot win if he loses his nerve. He should be self-confident and self-reliant and even if he does not win, he will know he has done his best.

- A chieftain does not have to be brilliant to be successful, but he must have an insatiable hunger for victory, absolute belief in his cause and an invincible courage that enables him to resist those who would otherwise discourage him.

- Seldom are self-centered, conceited and self-admiring chieftains great leaders, but they are great idolizers of themselves.

- Great chieftains never take themselves too seriously.

- A wise chieftain adapts—he doesn't compromise.

- Chieftains who drink with their Huns become one with them and are no longer their chieftain.

- Weak chieftains surround themselves with weak Huns.

- Strong chieftains surround themselves with strong Huns.

- As a chieftain achieves greater success, the jealousy others feel for him intensifies.

# COURAGE

- Huns must learn early that working through a hardship is an experience that influences them all the days of their lives.

- Successful Huns learn to deal with adversity and to overcome mistakes.

- A Hun can achieve anything for which he is willing to pay the price. Competition thins out at the top of the ranks.

# DECISION MAKING

- Every decision involves some risk.

- Time does not always improve a situation for a king or his Huns.

- Fundamental errors are inescapable when the unqualified are allowed to exercise judgment and make decisions.

- Quick decisions are not always the best decisions. On the other hand, unhurried decisions are not always the best decisions.

- Chieftains should never rush into confrontations.

- A chieftain's confidence in his decision making preempts name-dropping to his Huns.

- It is unfortunate when final decisions are made by chieftains headquartered miles away from the front, where they can only guess at conditions and potentialities known only to the captain on the battlefield.

- When victory will not be sweet, the chieftain must keep his Huns from war.

- The ability to make difficult decisions separates chieftains from Huns.

## DELEGATION

- Wise chieftains never place their Huns in situations where their weaknesses will prevail over their strengths.

- Good Huns normally achieve what their chieftain expects from them.

- A wise chieftain never expects his Huns to act beyond their wisdom and understanding.

- A wise chieftain always gives tough assignments to Huns who can rise to the occasion.

- Abdication is not delegation. Abdication is a sign of weakness. Delegation is a sign of strength.

## DEVELOPING CHIEFTAINS

- Strong chieftains always have strong weaknesses. A king's duty is to make a chieftain's strengths prevail.

- Huns learn less from success than they do from failure.

- Huns learn much faster when faced with adversity.

- A good chieftain takes risks by delegating to an inexperienced Hun in order to strengthen his leadership abilities.

- The experience of Huns must be structured to allow them to broaden and deepen themselves to develop the character they will need when appointed a chieftain.

- Huns are best prepared to become chieftains when given appropriate challenges at successively higher levels of responsibility.

- If it were easy to be a chieftain, everyone would be one.

- Without challenge, a Hun's potential is never realized.

- Appropriate stress is essential in developing chieftains.

## DIPLOMACY AND POLITICS

- When in a political war, a Hun must always keep an eye to the rear.

- The essence of Hunnish victory lies in the answers to the questions Where? and When?

- Huns should engage only in wars they can win.

- Huns may enter war as the result of failed diplomacy; however, war may be necessary for diplomacy to begin.

- For Huns, conflict is a natural state.

- Huns only make enemies on purpose.

- Huns never take by force what can be gained by diplomacy.

- Chieftains should remember that hospitality, warmth and courtesy will captivate even the most oppressive foe.

- Chieftains are often betrayed by those they trust most.

## GOALS

- Superficial goals lead to superficial results.

- As a nation, we would accomplish more if Huns behaved as though national goals were as important to them as personal goals.

- Critical to a Hun's success is a clear understanding of what the king wants.

- A Hun's goals should always be worthy of his efforts.

- A Hun without a purpose will never know when he has achieved it.

- A Hun's conformance does not always result in desired performance.

- Chieftains should always aim high, going after things that will make a difference rather than seeking the safe path of mediocrity.

## LEADERS AND LEADERSHIP

- Kings should always appoint their best Huns as chieftains, no matter how much they are needed in their current position.

- Never appoint acting chieftains. Put the most capable Hun in charge, give him both responsibility and authority, then hold him accountable.

- A wise chieftain never depends on luck. Rather, he always trusts his future to hard work, stamina, tenacity and a positive attitude.

- A wise chieftain knows he is responsible for the welfare of his Huns and acts accordingly.

- Being a leader of the Huns is often a lonely job.

- Once committed to action, chieftains must press for victory, not for stalemate—and surely not for compromise.

- Shared risk-taking will weld the relationship of a chieftain and his Huns.

- Strong chieftains stimulate and inspire the performance of their Huns.

- The best chieftains develop the ability to ask the right questions at the right time.

- A chieftain can never be in charge if he rides in the rear.

## PERCEPTIONS AND PUBLICITY

- In tough times, the nation will always call the meanest chieftain to lead.

- A Hun who takes himself too seriously has lost his perspective.

- A Hun's perception is reality for him.

- Huns who appear to be busy are not always working.

- It is best if your friends and foes speak well of you; however, it is better for them to speak poorly of you than not at all. When nothing can be said of a Hun, he has probably accomplished nothing very well.

- Contrary to what most chieftains think, you're not remembered by what you did in the past, but by what most Huns think you did.

## PERSONAL ACHIEVEMENT

- There is more nobility in being a good Hun than in being a poor chieftain.

- Even the Romans have the strength to endure the misfortunes they bring on others.

- If all Huns were blind, a one-eyed warrior would be king.

- Great chieftains accept failure at some things in order to excel in more important ones.

- Every Hun is responsible for shaping his life's circumstances and experiences into success—no other Hun, and certainly no Roman, can do for a Hun what he neglects to do for himself.

## PROBLEMS AND SOLUTIONS

- Huns should be taught to focus on opportunities rather than on problems.

- Some Huns have solutions for which there are no problems.

## REWARD AND PUNISHMENT

- If an incompetent chieftain is removed, seldom do we appoint his highest-ranking subordinate to his place. For when a chieftain has failed, so likewise have his subordinate leaders.

- If you tell a Hun he is doing a good job when he isn't, he will not listen long and, worse, will not believe praise when it is justified.

## TOLERANCE

- Every Hun has value—even if only to serve as a bad example.

- The error in appointing an incompetent chieftain is in leaving him in a position of authority over other Huns.

- To experience the strength of chieftains we must tolerate some of their weaknesses.

- Suffer long for mediocre but loyal Huns. Suffer not for competent but disloyal Huns.

## TRAINING

- Adequate training of Huns is essential to war and cannot be disregarded by chieftains in more peaceful times.

■ Teachable skills are for developing Huns. Learnable skills are reserved for chieftains.

■ The consequence for not adequately training your Huns is their failure to accomplish that which is expected of them.